SCHOLASTIC

Using Name Walls
to Teach Reading and Writing

Dozens of Classroom-Tested Ideas for Using This Motivating Tool to Teach
Phonological Awareness, Letter Recognition, Decoding, Spelling, and More

Janiel Wagstaff

New York • Toronto • London • Auckland • Sydney
Mexico City • New Delhi • Hong Kong • Buenos Aires

Teaching *Resources*

Dedication

For my real-life prince, Max, the best work I've ever done!

Acknowledgments

Thanks to:
Mom—without your help this book couldn't have been written;
Dad—thanks for always sharing Mom!
Joanna Davis-Swing, Terry Cooper, and *Virginia Dooley*—
for affording me another opportunity to share my literacy thinking.

For information on workshops and presentations or to contact Janiel,
write to: janielwag@hotmail.com or phone (801)546-6009.

Cover design by Holly Grundon
Interior design by Sarah Morrow
Interior photographs by Janiel Wagstaff

Copyright © 2009 by Janiel Wagstaff
All rights reserved. Published by Scholastic Inc.
Printed in the U.S.A.
ISBN-13: 978-0-545-10834-8
ISBN-10: 0-545-10834-9

1 2 3 4 5 6 7 8 9 10   40   15 14 13 12 11 10 09

Contents

Dear Colleague,

I was first struck by the awesome power of using students' names for learning years ago, while I was teaching kindergarten. In November, Stefan entered my class after his family was rescued from war-torn Bosnia by Catholic Relief Services. To give you an idea of the situation, Stefan's dad had shrapnel in his shoulder, and the family made their escape with only one suitcase. The suitcase was lost at the airport in New York, so they were beginning their lives in the U.S. with nothing. Luckily, the community stepped in to help with necessities, and they were set up in a tiny apartment near our school. Stefan came to me without knowing a single word of English. I could not communicate with his family because of the language barrier. Needless to say, we were all facing many challenges. Where would I begin?

Our kindergarten class had already built a Name Wall and was using it to practice phonological awareness and to learn and apply the ABCs (see Wagstaff, 1997, 1999, & 2001). As you would expect, when Stefan entered our room, we spent a lot of time introducing him to the class. We added his name and picture to the Name Wall the very first day.

Nothing extraordinary was done to encourage Stefan to pay any more attention to the Name Wall than any other student. He simply was immersed in our daily literacy activities, which included practice activities with the names on the Wall and constant reference to the Wall during modeled, shared, guided, and independent reading and writing. What became Stefan's first words in English (besides "yes" and "no")? His classmates' names! Before he could say them, he could point to their pictures on the Wall. Once he could voice them, they became his anchor words for learning the ABCs.

I stress the idea of making analogies in my teaching. On many occasions, Stefan would see an alphabet letter in a big book or other print and shout something like, "B! B! Brian!" Unsurprisingly, the students loved this! They would clap and cheer for him. Getting to know the students' names, then connecting these to the letter names, was his first step toward reading and writing. Scientific evidence points to the importance of learning letter names. "Among the readiness skills that are traditionally evaluated, the one that appears to be the strongest predictor (of later reading) on its own is letter identification" (Snow, Burns, & Griffin, 1998). The Name Wall definitely helped Stefan begin his journey into literacy.

Throughout my years of teaching, I've never forgotten the impact the Name Wall had on Stefan and other students who began school with little or no letter knowledge and/or were English language learners. As I've changed grades, moved from state to state, and had various teaching responsibilities with a host of different populations, I've developed numerous ways to capitalize on the natural motivation and fun provided by names.

Linking new learning to students' names has great potential for all kinds of literacy teaching. In this book, you'll see how to:

- use students' names to teach phonological awareness including rhyming; understanding and manipulating beginning, ending, and medial sounds in words; blending and segmenting;

- use students' names to teach letter names, letter forms, and letter sounds, as well as how to use them in everyday reading and writing;

- use students' names to teach chunks (spelling patterns) and how to use them to read and write new words; *and . . .*

- create dynamic Name Walls to support this learning while promoting application in multiple literacy contexts across the curriculum.

I focus on kid-friendly, concrete methods that infuse purpose with practice so that students know why they're doing what they're doing. The book is full of guided spelling and guided decoding experiences to help children develop strategic knowledge they can immediately use in everyday reading and writing. It all adds up to powerful learning across developmental stages K–2. As you study the lessons and employ the strategies, I'm confident you'll enjoy great success and have a lot of fun bringing literacy learning to life with names!

Best to you and your readers and writers,

Janiel Wagstaff

Introduction

Word Walls have been widely adopted in K–2 classrooms. The benefits of using a Word Wall every day are manyfold (adapted from Wagstaff, 1999).

Word Walls provide purposeful repetition required for real learning

Using Word Walls for explicit teaching and practice and in everyday reading and writing builds in the repetition many learners require for mastery. Consider the research table below. Without repeated exposures, many learners are left with incomplete knowledge toward the learning goal.

Think of this common scenario: in many classrooms, students are given a list of spelling words on Monday. Let's say the list consists of several words with two or three chunks to be learned. Students practice these words during the week, then take the test on Friday. They may earn 100 on the test, but if they don't repeatedly use the words and chunks, they are easily

Number of Exposures Needed to Learn a New Word

Level of Intelligence	IQ	Required Exposures
Significantly above average	120–129	20
Above average	110–119	30
Average	90–109	35
Slow learner	80–89	40
Mild cognitive impairment	70–79	45
Moderate cognitive impairment	60–69	55

Source: McCormick (1999)

forgotten. Our brighter students may retain the skill after a few exposures. But most students need more practice over time. Of course, this holds true for mastering word parts (letter-sound correspondences or chunks) for use in decoding as well. Using the Word Wall is a purposeful way of building in all those necessary repeated exposures!

Related research shows that seeing a word over and over in print is an effective way to master its spelling (Henderson & Chard, 1980). Adams (1990) concludes, "We should habitually encourage students to look at (the) spelling patterns . . . we want them to learn" (p. 396). You can check this off your instructional agenda as a consequence of constant referencing and involvement in Word Wall activities!

Word Walls provide ongoing, concrete, easily accessible support for struggling learners

Teachers often ask when to "retire" words from the Wall. I always say, don't take words down from the Walls because by doing so, you're hurting the students who need them the most: the struggling literacy learners. Instead, be picky about which words are added to the Walls, so you're not "swimming in words," and use effective techniques for economizing space and providing accessibility (these will be described below).

Word Walls enhance contextualized learning through practical use

The real power of Word Walls lies in their practical use every day across a variety of reading and writing experiences. Lots of teachers put words on a wall and use them for wordplay activities. Though this builds in some of the useful repetition noted with the first benefit; the rubber hits the road when students are asked to apply the skills and strategies they're learning in authentic reading and writing contexts. I use the Walls incessantly as I model reading and writing to strategize using one word to read or write another or to check that I've used a word or word part correctly. We refer to them continually during shared and guided experiences, too. Demonstrations coupled with rich, explicit guided spelling and guided decoding practice are key to success. Then, I look for students' use of the skills and strategies in their own reading and writing. Showing knowledge of letter sounds or chunks in an isolated exercise is one thing. Demonstrating that same knowledge while reading a book or writing a story is quite another. That's the kind of rich learning I'm looking for, and using the Word Walls facilitates that kind of teaching and practice.

Reflect on This

In kindergarten classrooms, students are often drilled on letter identification and sounds then tested on their mastery. This is an important learning goal, but in the end, it's students' abilities to use those letters and sounds in their emergent reading and writing that matters. The transition from isolated practice to real application doesn't come naturally for all. But, if I teach these same skills with the help of a Word Wall, then model and provide guided practice using the letters and sounds to accomplish real reading and writing tasks, students' overall literacy abilities flourish.

Word Walls encourage the use of references to independently solve problems

Once students learn to use the Wall to problem solve, they can do so independently and even provide help for classmates. Recently, I happily watched as one bilingual student translated how to use a name on the Wall for another student with very limited English proficiency. That's empowering!

Note

There is one exception to this. When the goal is to get students to master irregular high-frequency words, the choice of which words go on the Wall does matter. After all, only certain words fit into the irregular and high-frequency category (like said *and* they*). For more information on this, see the chapter on the* Words We Know Wall *in my book* Teaching Reading and Writing With Word Walls *(1999).*

Word Walls are easily integrated into any literacy program and all daily literacy activities

I'll show how to use your students' names as potent first Word Wall words. After that, you can use words from any source to expand your Walls. For example, the vocabulary words in your district's reading program or the spelling words from your language program can be used as Word Wall words. The trick is to show students how to use the word parts in the familiar words to read and write new words. It's not the actual words or the number of words on the Wall that's important, although it is true some chunks are more useful than others (see Note at left). Instead, it's what you draw attention to and how you guide students in using the words that makes a real difference in their reading and writing. And, it's easy to reference the Wall during any literacy activity, whether it be one from an established literacy program or something you're reading and writing in science or social studies. You'll see how to do that throughout this book.

In addition to the above, there are unique benefits to building and using a Name Wall in your classroom:

Names are important

We know motivation and relevance are essential to learning. When using students' names, motivation and relevance are naturally built right in. Students have interest in each other's names given our social natures.

Using names is already part of curriculum

Educators know the importance of building strong communities in classrooms. One method for doing so is designing activities around students' names. Building a Name Wall is an easy extension of this work and it really pays off. It can be used for fruitful learning all year!

Names have built-in mastery

Is there a student in your class who does not know his or her classmates names? I've never had one. Students have to be familiar with the words on the Wall to use them to read and write new words. With the Name Wall, that familiarity is built right in. Struggling literacy learners master the phonological awareness skills, letter-sound correspondences and spelling patterns in names with greater ease since the words used in lessons are already familiar and meaningful. The same is true for English language learners. Often, the first words they master are classmates' names. Working with names as described herein makes a host of literacy skills more accessible for this population.

Using names takes advantage of how the brain learns

The brain learns by connecting the new to the known. So, meaningful association makes learning less arduous. It's easy to attach new learning to well known names. they're very powerful anchors making them perfect first Word Wall words! When students get off to a good start, their chances of overall success skyrocket since they're likely to read and write more. Using names helps make that happen.

When teachers consider the idea of a Name Wall the first question they ask is "How do I use *my* students' names?" Yes, every year, you'll have a different class roster. But, many of the basic literacy skills in your grade-level curriculum can be taught and reinforced with your students' names no matter what they are. You can't beat the efficiency and power of using names to jump-start learning concepts and skills. I'll show you how throughout the book.

CHAPTER 1

ABC Name Walls for Phonological Awareness

Here, from *The Art of Teaching Writing* (Calkins, 1994), a first-grade teacher is talking to one of her students:

> *"Do you want to write something?" Martha asked her, but Renee didn't seem to understand. Martha tried again. "Can you say* Santa *slowly, listening to the sounds?" Soon, Martha and Renee were sounding out* S-s-s-s-s-anta. *"What sounds do you hear?" Renee whispered the word to herself again, listening intently to it, "Sa-a-nta," she said. Then she looked proudly at Martha and announced, "I hear* Ho, ho, ho" *(p. 90).*

True, Renee can't segment a word into sounds. Even more disturbing, she clearly has no understanding of what she's being asked to do or why it's important. This scenario perfectly illustrates why some children have difficulty with phonological awareness. Since they've been hearing and using words for meaning since birth, they can miss the whole idea that words are made up of abstract, meaningless sounds.

As kindergarten and first-grade teachers, we have to be sure all our students develop phonological awareness so scenarios like Renee's don't happen. Certainly, science has proven the critical nature of the ability to work with the sounds making up words (Adams, 1990; Snow et al., 1998; Armbruster, Lehr, & Osborn, 2001). Teachers know students who can rhyme; match beginning, middle and ending sounds; segment words into sounds; and blend sounds into words have the base necessary to understand what letters represent. In fact, most can tell you that phonemic awareness has been shown to be one of the strongest predictors of students' future abilities to read and write (Adams, 1990; Snow et al., 1998).

> **Note**
>
> *Be sure to review the key terms in the appendix if the concept of phonological awareness is new to you.*

Phonological awareness is an issue in second grade and beyond as well, particularly for struggling literacy learners. During my years with second graders and working as a literacy specialist with below-level readers in grades 3–6, I found many of my strugglers lacked basic phonemic awareness skills they should have developed in kindergarten and first grade. Additionally, many English language learners experience difficulty hearing and manipulating sounds in English words. Accordingly, we should all be concerned with phonological awareness.

The emphasis on scientifically proven practices and proliferation of "The Federal Five" brought on by No Child Left Behind legislation has highlighted the importance of phonological awareness. Many school districts use DIBELS measures (Good & Kaminski, 2002) as one indication of students' adequate yearly progress. Both of these facts serve us well, since many classrooms lacked a clear phonological awareness focus before, and DIBELS is a fast, easy screening measure. However, educators have to remember that phonological awareness is not an end in itself. We do not practice rhyming, matching, segmenting, blending, and other manipulation of sounds simply because we want students to be good at those things and meet the DIBELS benchmarks. In short, our aim should *not* simply be to have students master phonological awareness tasks. Rather, our instructional approaches should overtly reflect that we build these abilities so students may fully benefit from our phonics instruction to become more proficient readers and writers (Adams et al., 1998; Armbruster et al., 2001).

As a literacy specialist assisting schools in a very large school district, I've seen plenty of phonological awareness practice done in isolation. In these classrooms, it seems, getting a certain score on a simple measure is the end goal. Yet there is no reason to teach in isolation. Students do much better when they know why they're learning what they're learning.

The implications for curriculum are clear. We should design practice activities to help students build proficiency with phonological tasks while couching them within literacy programs where students are immersed in real reading and writing from day one. When we model, instruct, and provide guided and independent practice, we must constantly show the connections of those practices to students' total literacy.

One reason I love Name Walls is that they enable teachers to do just that. We can teach and practice rhyming, matching, isolating, substituting, segmenting, and blending sounds with students' names *and* we can post the names to boost facility with letter-sound correspondences. Then, we make use of the Wall in everyday reading and writing. It really is that easy!

> *Note*
>
> Research indicates that the most effective approach (to phonemic awareness instruction) is a combination of direct sound-work activities and attention to print, including the learning of letter-sound correspondences (IRA, 1998; Snow et al., 1998; Armbruster et al., 2001).

Grade-Level Relevance

Since we primarily teach phonological awareness in kindergarten and first grade, the Name Wall described in this chapter is designed for that age group. However, beginning English language learners of any age will benefit from its use. Work with this Wall continues in Chapter 2, and in

Chapters 3 and 4, you'll see the identical organization used for reinforcing letter-sound correspondences. This way, we take advantage of the reciprocal nature of phonological awareness and phonics by teaching them simultaneously. Learning letter-sound correspondences increases understanding of how sounds work in words, while learning how sounds work in words facilitates learning and applying letter-sound correspondences. Yopp (1992) puts it this way, ". . . phonemic awareness is both a prerequisite for and a consequence of learning to read."

If you teach second graders or older students, or English language learners in the developing stage, I recommend organizing the Name Wall by chunks (see Chapters 5 and 6). Even though the organization of the Wall is different, you can use your students' names exactly as described here to help your strugglers develop phonemic awareness if needed.

Getting Started: Building the ABC Name Wall

Physical Construction

Over the years, I've experimented with building Word Walls many different ways. I'm completely sold on using one material for ease, mobility, and durability: foam boards.

Foam boards are also called display boards. They can be purchased at office supply stores and are available in many sizes and colors. Sizes range from 20 in. x 30 in. to 60 in. x 40 in. Made of a sturdy layer of foam with a paper covering on each side, they can be propped up or leaned against chairs or walls for placement anywhere in the classroom. Last year, I propped up mine on a low bookshelf unit, then had students move them to the front chalk trays for instruction and use during Reading and Writing Workshop. They stand on the floor for hands-on accessibility and can be used to section off a place in the room for a center. I've used the same boards for my Word Walls for almost ten years. They're a little bent around the edges, but they've stood up beautifully to a lot of wear and tear!

As a literacy specialist working with different groups of children, I even use both sides of the foam boards. For example, I have a Name Wall for my first-grade group on one side and my second-grade group on the other. I just turn the Wall around to work with each group. Half-day kindergarten teachers do the same. A.M. words are on one side, P.M. on the other. This is a great space and resource saver!

Affixing Words to the Walls

I prefer using Velcro to affix words to the Wall. Words can easily be removed for use in lessons or centers or by students at their desks, then re-posted with minimal effort. The Velcro backing simply stays on the Wall from year to year, while the other part stays on the word card (makes for very easy on, easy off!).

Name Cards for the Walls

Before school starts, I cut multicolored pieces of cardstock into three-inch wide strips. I write students' names (one per card) with black marker in bold letters. I underline the letter(s) representing the beginning sound for the ABC Name Wall for kindergarten and first grade. A chunk is underlined in each name for the Chunking Name Wall for second grade and beyond. Additionally, I cut around the shape of the letters as shown. The cardstock will last all year without being laminated, even when the cards are used on and off the Wall.

Figure 1.1 *ABC Name Wall student pictures and name cards*

Building the Walls

On the first day of school, I take students' pictures with a digital camera, then print and trim the photos. Then, we spend the first week adding students' pictures to the Wall (five to seven each day) and discussing how their names will be used. In my book *Teaching Reading and Writing With Word Walls* (1999), I argue for the need to use a literacy context such as a rhyme, poem, or chant to choose key words, then to add just a few words each week to the Wall. This gradual process allows students to become familiar with the words and the context serves to make

Figure 1.2 *Name Chunking Wall student picture and name card*

the words more memorable. I don't have the same concerns about names, since they are so very well known. They truly are in a class of words by themselves.

Knowing this, I feel comfortable posting all the photos and names quickly and getting right to work constantly modeling their usefulness. I prefer this approach, since I can get in a great deal of incidental teaching right from the start. Then, each week, we focus on a few names for intense practice. Later, we cover more phonics ground by studying and posting additional words to our Walls. At that time, I apply the principles I wrote about before to ensure success. You'll see how this works when we address extending the Walls, pacing, and weekly schedules.

If you prefer, post a few names each week for a more gradual approach. Remember, no matter what approach you take, a few names will be chosen each week for in-depth study; other words will be added later in the year.

If you choose to take more time, post names with the least confusing letter sounds first. For example, go ahead and post Manuel, Mindy, Lateefa, Lincoln, Sara, and Stetson early on since they start with continuous sounds (speech sounds with an uninterrupted flow) and the sound the first letter makes in each name is identical. Wait to post names like Cathy, Cindy and Charles, Adam, Adrien and Amari, Jose and Jennifer since they have varied beginning sounds. If you are a half-day kindergarten teacher who works two sessions, simply put one class on the front and the other on the back of your foam board.

Figure 1.3 *Partial ABC Name Wall before additions of new words (other than names) are made. (Bart was our class pet and Cubby was our traveling, journaling bear.) Notice that* Danielle *and* Dominica *are aligned perfectly vertically, since the beginning sound is identical in both names.* Adam, Adrien, *and* Aubrie *are misaligned because the beginning sound is different in each.* Juanita *is positioned between the* J *and* K *names because it begins with the letter* J *but has an unusual sound.*

Organizing the ABC Name Wall

The ABC Name Wall is organized in alphabetical order, but what about letters with different sounds? The names are posted in a perfectly vertical line only if the underlined letter sound is exactly the same from name to name. One year, I had three kindergartners whose names began with the letter *a*, but all had a different beginning sound. As you can see in the figures above, I place them under the letter *a* as they are all spelled with *a*, but I don't sort them vertically. Instead, they are a bit off-centered to distinguish one sound from another. The same is true for names like *Juanita*. She's positioned between the letters *j* and *k*, since her name starts with *j*, but represents an unusual sound. Consonant digraphs and long and short vowels are handled the same way. *Charlie* is just to the side of the hard and soft *c* names, *Shauntelle* is alongside the *s* names, while *Enrique* and *Elizabeth* are positioned to separate long and short *e* groups.

Extending Your ABC Name Wall Beyond Your Class Names

I've never had a roster of names starting with every letter. You might exercise these options to cover the whole alphabet and other critical sounds (consonant digraphs, hard and soft consonants, long and short vowels):

- Add names of favorite characters from books, names of prominent people in your school, names of class pets or mascots, and so on. Add *just one* to use as your consistent reference for each sound.

- Add one key word taken from a book, song, rhyme, poem, or chant to represent each sound your students' names don't cover. I choose this route since I can use the rhymes, poems, and chants for shared reading, then give kids copies for independent rereading,

Figure 1.4 *Here's the same section of the ABC Wall now with additions of other words harvested from poems, rhymes, and chants.* Chicka *was added from the book* Chicka Chicka Boom Boom, five *was added from the book* Five Little Monkeys, gum *was added from the rhyme "Bubble Gum, Bubble Gum, in a dish . . . ," and* happy *was added from the song "If You're Happy and You Know It." Additions like these are made over time. Notice that* chicka *is placed between* c *and* d *since it begins with the letter* c *but the digraph* ch *represents its own sound.*

thereby integrating curriculum. (For more information on working with words harvested from engaging literacy contexts, see my book *Teaching Reading and Writing With Word Walls* (1999). If you're using an adopted reading program, keep in mind these words can come from those materials.

Examples: The mean substitute teacher, Viola Swamp, from *Miss Nelson Is Missing* is a memorable character, making hers a super name to add to your ABC Name Wall for the /v/ sound. *Chicka* from *Chicka Chicka Boom Boom* sticks in the brain from the fun refrain in the book, so it's a great example of a memorable word to add if you find you need one for /ch/.

Since I'm advocating teaching phonological awareness simultaneously with letter sounds, it makes sense to extend the ABC Name Wall beyond students' names as just described, so all critical correspondences are covered. If you're not sure which letter sounds to include, cross-check what's on your Wall with the phonics scope and sequence for your grade level (either from your adopted reading program or your state standards). Then, make the appropriate additions at a pace that makes sense for your students and their growing abilities. Keep in mind, as the Wall grows, you're still continually using the sounds and correspondences already posted, so practice and review are built right in. Here's a general guideline for additions:

> **Note**
>
> Once we begin adding words other than names to our Wall, we simply call it the ABC Wall.

Pacing Guide for Extending Your Wall

In kindergarten: Add two words each week. It's a good idea to post a picture cue next to each word to lend more support for emergent learners.

In first grade: Because you are "reviewing" the alphabet, add three words per week at first; then assess students' mastery of the posted correspondences if you want to increase the pace. It's beneficial to strugglers and second-language learners to include picture cues.

Why post just *one* key word per additional letter-sound correspondence beyond those represented by your students' names? When you come back to that same word all year long, you're building in the repetition needed for mastery. Plus, posting just one reference for a word part forces students to use the analogy strategies. Though it's a useful activity to do a word hunt, for the /ch/ sound for example, I wouldn't post all those words on my Wall. If you do, you'll be swimming in words, making it difficult to reference. And, if students can just copy a /ch/ word they need from a list, they won't apply strategies. Instead, stick with just one consistent reference, like *chicka*. If you're using your Wall daily, you'll be amazed at how many times you'll refer to these same words and how well your students will get to know them. You'll see, it really works!

When might you begin extending your ABC Name Wall beyond the letter sounds included in your students' names? One way of testing your students' mastery of the letter sounds already posted (once you've thoroughly worked with them, of course) is to turn the Word Wall around to the blank side and probe what they can do without support. For example, in kindergarten, you might say the names and ask children to write the beginning letter. In first grade, you might ask them to record letters for all the sounds they hear in the names once they've written the first letter sound. This is a great way to assess phonemic awareness too, since children can hear and distinguish what they are able to represent with letters. Instead, or in addition, you can use a letter-recognition test, having students name the letter and produce a sound for the posted correspondences. It won't be necessary for all students to have mastered all the letter sounds posted on the Wall before extending it, since practice with what's posted will continue. Remember, we don't retire words from our Walls, so those who need more time have it. However, you should feel confident you're not overwhelming students by adding more if most are clearly still learning the letter sounds already on the Wall. You may be surprised, though, as I've been in teaching varied groups around the country, at how quickly students master the letter sounds in their classmates' names!

The Ultimate Goal

The ultimate goal of any Word Wall is to put itself out of business. It serves as a learning tool. We work with, then post, the names to make it easier for students to learn letter sounds and chunks by meaningful association. We teach strategic thinking—how to make connections to word parts on the Wall to read and write new words. All of this is done in all kinds of literacy contexts, all day long, every day, on the journey toward automaticity. The more we review and work with the words and their parts, the more automatic they become. Once they're automatic, students no longer need to refer to the Wall. In the end, children are more skillful and proficient, and they have the strategic thinking they need to solve reading and writing problems. Word Walls are well worth the effort!

Introducing the ABC Name Wall for Phonological Awareness

Think back to what happened when first grader Renee attempted to hear the sounds in the word *Santa* on page 12. Obviously, her confusion about the concept of sounds in words will hold back her literacy progress. From the very start, we want our instruction to be crystal clear to students. When introducing the ABC Name Wall the first week of school, I make sure to be explicit about why we are building it and how we will use it. Concrete models are an integral part of the instruction, so abstract phonological awareness concepts are made kid-friendly and completely understandable. I begin by emphasizing using our names to understand how sounds work in words followed by some brief practice. Within a few days, I add how we'll use the names for reading and writing (See Introducing the ABC Name Wall to Build Letter–Sound Knowledge in Chapter 3, page 47).

I say to students,

> Words have meanings. We all know this. We've been hearing words since we were born. When we hear a word, we can't help but think of its meaning. For example, if I say the word *horse*, you picture a horse in your mind and you think about what you know about horses. But there is something else you need to know about words. Words are made up of sounds. These sounds have no meaning at all. They are simply the parts we voice when we move our mouths and tongues and push air through to say words. The word *horse* is made up of three sounds: /h/ /or/ /s/. These sounds have nothing to do with an actual horse. Let me show you what I mean with something you are all familiar with: Mat's name.
>
> When I say Mat's name, you automatically think of Mat because you know him. But, here's something else we can learn about Mat's name. As I say it, I'm voicing three sounds. Watch . . .

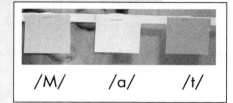

Figure 1.5 *Segmenting M-a-t*

I stretch an elastic model (see Figure 1.5) and articulate each sound separately moving from right to left with my lips under the pieces of cardstock as they are pulled apart. (See instructions in Note on page 21.)

Note

When you move from right to left as you face the class, students see the correct model—from left to right.

> Now you can actually *see* how Mat's name is made up of three sounds. Again, the sounds don't have any meaning themselves and they can be hard to hear and pull apart since we're so used to saying them smushed together in Mat's name. Say the sounds with me again as I stretch his name and the elastic. /Mmmmm/ /aaaaa/ /ttttt/. See? Here is the first, middle, and last sound in Mat's name [*I point to each piece of cardstock and voice the sounds again*]. Watch and listen again. /Mmmm/ /aaaaa/ /ttttt/.
>
> Now, let's try it together again. You have to be able to hear the sounds in words to be able to write them. If I can't break a word into its sounds, I can't figure out the letters I need to write it. This is important for reading, too. When I sound out letters, I have to be able to blend, or smush, those sounds together to make a word. Watch . . . [*I contract the stretched elastic while blending the sounds together*] /Mat/! Watch again, /m/ /a/ /t/ [*I use my nose to point to each card*]

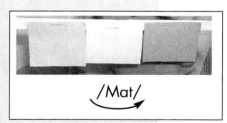

Figure 1.6 *Blending M-a-t*

are blended together to make the name /Mat/ [*I contract the stretched elastic again*]! Knowing how sounds work in words is very important to us as readers and writers. I'll tell you more about that later.

Now, let's practice hearing sounds in each other's names. As we work, you'll find all of our names are made up of little sounds. When you know this is true and you can hear these sounds, you'll start to see how the same sounds in our names are in lots of other words.

After modeling segmenting and blending the phonemes in several names, involving students as much as possible, give them some guided practice. You can make elastic models for pairs to use as you direct them. Or, try this: Give each student one pipe cleaner and four 9 x 6 mm plastic "pony" beads (these slide on and off the pipe cleaner easily, but also stay securely in one place once positioned). Each brightly colored bead represents a phoneme, so the number of beads needed depends on the number of phonemes in the longest name you'll use for practice. Keep in mind, working with smaller words with fewer sounds is easier than working with larger words with more sounds.

Start by working with names with the fewest phonemes:

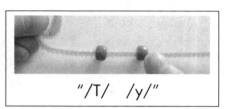
"/T/   /y/"

Figure 1.7 *Beads on a pipe cleaner*

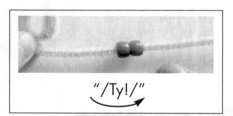
"/Ty!/"

Figure 1.8 *Blending with beads*

Great Trick

Use different-color beads to represent different sounds in varied positions within the names. For example, a yellow bead can represent the beginning (or first) sound, a blue bead the middle sound, a red bead the ending (or last) sound, and so on.

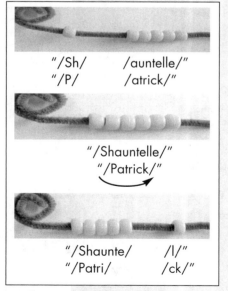
"/Sh/   /auntelle/"
"/P/   /atrick/"

"/Shauntelle/"
"/Patrick/"

"/Shaunte/   /l/"
"/Patri/   /ck/"

Figure 1.9 *Practicing segmenting and blending beginning and ending sounds*

Let's try to hear all the sounds in Ty's name. [*Demonstrate listening inside the name for phonemes stretching an elastic model with two pieces of cardstock.*] How many sounds do you hear?

Two! students reply.

Yes, Ty's name has two sounds. Watch again: /Ttttt/ /yyyyy/ [*stretch the band while segmenting*], /Ty!/ [*contract the band while blending*]. Now say it with me as I do it again.

You can make your own model of the two sounds in Ty's name. Take your pipe cleaner and roll one end up like this. [*Demonstrate as you give directions.*] This end will keep the beads from falling off. We are going to string one bead for each sound we hear. How many sounds does Ty's name have?

Two! students reply.

Right! So, string two different colored beads to show two different sounds. /Ttttt/ [*string one bead*], /yyyyy/ [*string the other*]. Move the beads to the middle of your pipe cleaner. Smush them right next to each other so the two sounds blend together to make Ty's name. Now, run your finger under them to read his name. (See Figure 1.7.)

/Ty/! Great!Now, let's listen inside Ty's name and say the sounds slowly, breaking them apart, voicing one at a time. Watch me, then you try. /Ttttt/ [*pull the first bead away from the second*], /yyyyy/ [*pull the second bead down a bit.*] See! We can see the first sound in Ty's name [*point to the first bead*] /ttttt/, and here's the last sound in Ty's name /yyyyy/ [*pointing to the second bead (see Figure 1.8)*]. Now, I'll smush them back together: /Ty/! Now, try it with me with your beads!

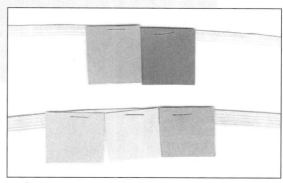

Figure 1.10 *First, an elastic model made for names with two phonemes, second a model for names with three phonemes*

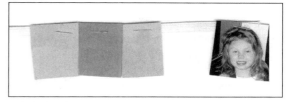

Figure 1.11 *This elastic model is designed for practicing the three phonemes in Lil's name: /l/ /i/ /l/.*

Allow students to practice segmenting and blending the beads in the same name several times before moving on to another name. During the first demonstration and practice sessions with kindergartners and beginning English language learners, I stick with names with just two or three phonemes. For longer names, we string more beads and segment off the beginning sound only, then smush it back together with the other beads to blend the name. (This works nicely for distinguishing ending sounds, too; see Figure 1.9.)

Initial experiences in first grade and with more developed English language learners may include more phonemes, depending on how students fare with two and three. The key for all grades and ability levels is to repeat these lessons several times, then use the pipe cleaner and other concrete models to demonstrate segmenting and blending when appropriate in daily reading and writing.

Introducing the ABC Name Wall for Phonological Awareness—Continued

Children may require several solid introductions to how sounds work in words. There's no substitute for ensuring they understand the concept since it underlies all we do with letters and sounds. This reminds me of Alberto, a kindergartner undergoing a phonemic awareness test:

Teacher: What's the first sound you hear in *bed*?

Alberto: [*tilts his head and responds*] Zzzzzzzzzzzzzzzzzz!

Note

Instructions for Making Elastic Models for Segmenting and Blending Phonemes

Staple pieces of cardstock side-by-side to strips of elastic waistband (found in sewing stores). You need one piece of cardstock to represent each phoneme within a word. To program models for specific students, staple a photo on the end. The waistband material lends itself to an analogy. We stretch the band in the same way we stretch out the sounds in words as we segment, then contract the band and smush or blend the sounds back together. Models can be used for instruction in whole and small groups and in centers or as take-homes.

Alberto's correct! A snore may be the first sound heard in bed! He's focusing on the meaning of bed and, like Renee, has serious confusion about what we mean by sounds in words.

Here's another useful demonstration, perfect for the first week of school, to make the concept concrete:

> Boys and girls, remember we were talking about how little sounds that don't have any meaning are smushed together in the words we say? We practiced using pipe cleaners strung with beads to hear the sounds inside each other's names, pulling the sounds apart and then blending them back together. Now I want to show you another example that will help you understand.
>
> When we talk, you can't see words come out of our mouths, right? Let's pretend for a moment we can. As I say the name *Becka*, pretend you *can* see it come out of my mouth. Ready? *Becka* [*as I say it, I bring a closed fist with four linked Unifix cubes to my mouth, then "pull" them out, showing them in my fingers*]. Watch again. Becka [*I repeat making the linked cubes appear to come out of my mouth*]. Since we can now see the word, let's listen inside it to hear its sounds. /Bbbbb/ [*I point to the first cube*], /eeeee/ [*I point to the next cube*], /kkk/ [*I point to the third cube*], /aaaaa/ [*I point to the last cube*]. The sounds that come together to make Becka's name can be broken apart: /B/ [*I pull off the first cube*], /e/ [*I pull off the next cube*], /ck/ [*I pull off the third cube*], /a/ [*showing the last cube*] and they can be put back together. [*I continuously voice the sounds, putting each piece (starting with the first cube) back together with the whole. Then I run my finger under the linked cubes:*] Becka!
>
> [*I repeat the demonstration, then propose:*] Let's see how this works with other names!

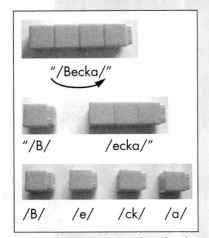

Figure 1.12 *Working with Unifix cubes*

Figure 1.13 *Pulling a word out of my mouth so it can be "seen"*

After I model segmenting and blending several names, it's time for guided practice. Students partner up and get three Unifix cubes. Starting with short names, those with two or three phonemes, students take turns repeating a name I say, using the Unifix cubes to represent the sounds. They "pull" the name out of their mouths (moving their fists up to, then away from their mouths), for the partners to see. Then, they work together to break the name apart into each of its sounds (pulling apart the Unifix cubes), then blending it back together. We work on one name at a time, as I provide explicit guidance. Partners switch roles with each new name.

As suggested with the pipe cleaner and beads, start with short names and repeat the lesson several times before working with names with more phonemes. Then, incorporate the use of Unifix cubes into daily literacy events.

Extending the Use of Concrete Models

The elastic models, pipe cleaners with beads, and Unifix cubes may be used to represent other word parts besides phonemes. Here are a number of examples proceeding from easier to more difficult. It is easier to work with larger units of sound (syllables, then onsets and rimes) than smaller units of sound (phonemes).

Hint

Laminate colored sheets of cardstock before you cut and staple to create elastic models. That way, you can use vis-à-vis markers to write on and wipe off letters for varied activities.

Syllable Level

I like to use different colors of cardstock, beads or Unifix cubes to represent each syllable (Figure 1.14). I also make models without photo cues so they may be used to represent lots of different multisyllabic words.

Segment and blend syllables with pipe cleaners and beads and Unifix cubes, too. Use one bead or cube for each syllable (Figure 1.15).

Additional Help for Teaching Syllables

In addition to having students clap, jump, or tap the syllables in words, try these helpful ideas:

1. have students place one hand under their chin to feel the jaw drop with each syllable
2. have them hum words to detect the syllables

Additionally, try referring to syllables as "beats" with young children.

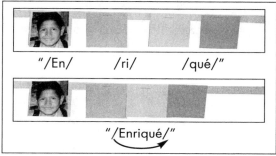

Figure 1.14 *Elastic with photo and cardstock squares representing syllables*

Onset/Rime Level

For the elastic models, I like to use different colors and sizes of cardstock to represent different word parts. In Figure 1.16, I cut a smaller piece of yellow cardstock to represent the /br/ onset (which is a smaller unit of sound) and a larger piece of blue cardstock to represent the /ent/ rime (the larger unit of sound). This way, the concept is represented visually in two forms: by color and by size.

Represent onsets and rimes with beads and Unifix cubes. Use one bead or cube for the onset and one bead or cube for the rime. Different colors for each word part are helpful (see Figure 1.17).

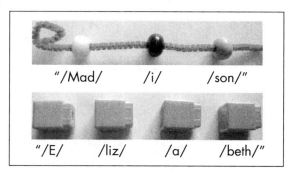

Figure 1.15 *Pipe cleaner with beads and Unifix cubes representing syllables*

Note

In some words, the onset and rime are the same size both in terms of the number of phonemes and the number of letters used to spell each part. For example, the word *my* has a single phoneme onset, spelled with one letter (m) and a single phoneme rime spelled with one letter (y). In cases like this, represent the word parts with the elastic models at the phoneme level, since each piece is the same size, or use the pipe cleaner or Unifix models on next page.

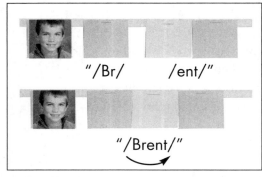

Figure 1.16 *Elastic model representing onset and rime*

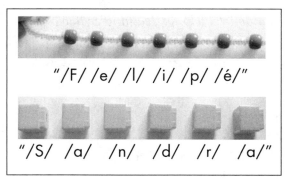

Figure 1.17 *Onset and rime with beads and cubes*

Phoneme Level

Again, different colors of cardstock, beads, or Unifix cubes can be used to represent each phoneme.

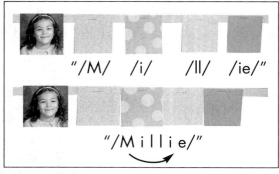

Figure 1.18 *Using concrete models to represent phonemes*

Making the Elastic Models for Rhyming

Many of us have students who have difficulty with the concept of rhyme. A visual model of what we mean by rhyme can be really helpful. I make the models the same way I do for demonstrating onset and rime, with a smaller piece of cardstock of one color representing the beginning sound(s) and a larger piece of a different color representing the rhyming portion of the word. While reading aloud a rhyming book, I explain this way:

> We've heard many rhyming words in this book. Let's go back and find some. Here are two rhyming words: *kiss* and *miss*. Say them with me: *kiss, miss*. Rhyming words sound the same at the end but have different beginning sounds. I'm going to listen inside *kiss* and *miss* for two parts and show them to you. See if you can tell what is the same and what is different.

I stretch the elastic and voice the beginning sound /k/ (with my mouth visible just underneath the cardstock as I point to it with my nose), then stretch it further and voice the rime /iss/ (again with my mouth visible underneath, pointing with my nose). Then, I contract the elastic to blend the sounds /kiss/. I repeat the procedure with *miss* and ask,

"Did you see the word parts? Which part is the same? That's right! The chunk of sound /iss/ is the same at the end of both words, while the beginning sounds are different. That's how rhyming words work! Did you notice how my mouth moves the same and makes the same shape at the end of both words? Watch. [*I voice the rime again, with the elastic stretched, pointing:*] /iss/ /iss/ /iss/. See how my teeth are tight together, and my lips are apart? That's another clue. Now, you try it with me.

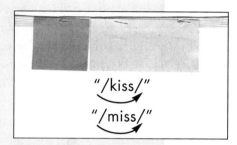

Figure 1.19 *Segmenting and blending rhyming words*

I use the model again as we compare *kiss* and *miss* for sound and feel. I also explain to students how the chunk of sound at the end is bigger than the beginning sound because it includes the vowel and what comes after. Visually, then, it makes sense to have a larger piece of cardstock for the rime. Again, adjust which model you use when the two parts are the same size.

We repeat the words, having students confirm the sound and feel of the rime:

Let's continue to look back in our book for more rhyming words. Then we'll test them with our elastic so we can see the parts that rhyme!

Repeat and test several rhyming words. Revisit this procedure frequently to build students' facility with rhyme. Use their names (if need be, make up nonsense rhyming words to compare), provide them with one word, then have them volunteer a word that rhymes (then compare the two with the model), and have those who need more practice meet with you in a small group, each child with his or her own elastic model to manipulate.

The pipe cleaners with beads and Unifix cube models may also be used to demonstrate and practice rhyming (one bead or cube is needed for the onset, one for the rime).

More Clues to Sounds: Mouth Positions

Couple using concrete models to "see" the sounds within words with having students notice how sounds "feel" when they're voiced, as shown in the rhyming lesson above. Phonemes have distinct mouth positions. For example, /m/, /p/, and /b/ are all produced with the lips closed and the latter two "pop" air out when they're voiced. For /f/ and /v/, our top teeth are on our bottom lip sending a slight stream of air downward. It's useful to develop characterizations for sounds with students' help by asking, "How would you describe what your mouth is doing as you make that sound?" You'll see I integrate these clues throughout my instruction. If you'd like to learn more, consult Lindamood & Lindamood (1998) and Blevins (2006). These resources include charts depicting mouth positions.

It's beneficial to give students small mirrors to see their mouth positions. If you don't have enough for each child, have them work in pairs, taking turns holding the mirror.

More Clever Concrete Models

I've had a great time over the years experimenting with other simple models for demonstrations and practice. Here are a number of my best ideas. You'll be pleased with how effectively they simplify your teaching while making concepts concrete and more comprehensible, thus learnable, for your students. Use these models to augment your direct explanation, then follow up with guided practice. They motivate independent practice in centers, too! Best of all, they really work! If you use them regularly, students will deeply understand these abstract concepts and have greater facility with sounds in words.

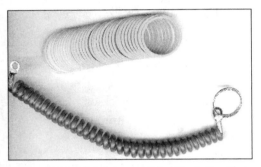

Figure 1.20 *Mini-slinky and Spiral Plastic Key Chain*

Figure 1.21 *Kid Smush*

Mini-Slinkies and Spiral Plastic Key Chains

Both of these can be purchased at variety stores that sell party supplies. Sometimes, dollar stores also carry them or you can search for them on the Internet (search for *mini plastic slinkies* and *key chains with spiral wristlets* or *spiral cords*). They're packaged in lots of about a half dozen. They are perfect for stretching apart to represent segmenting sounds and retracting to represent blending, just like the elastic models!

Kid Smush

Use your kids to represent the phonemes in names! When working with a word with three phonemes, for example, smush three volunteers together (they stand closely side-by-side with arms locked—arms are locked just like sounds seem locked together within a word). Run your hand over their heads in a smooth motion to represent the whole name as you say it, then dramatically tug each child away from the others to segment each sound ("Boy, those sounds can be hard to hear and pull apart!") Push them together again to blend the sounds back into the name.

Additionally, use Kid Smush as a model for the concept of rhyme. Have one child represent the beginning sound and two or three others represent the rime (these kids keep their arms locked together at all times, just like the chunk of sound at the end of rhyming words stays "locked" the same from word to word). Segment off the beginning sound (by pulling the first child away), then smush together to reblend with the rime. Play with changing the beginning sound to represent different rhyming words.

> **Hint**
>
> *Use* different *volunteers to represent the* different *beginning sounds!*

Kid Smush makes a great model for syllables, too! Using one child to represent each beat in a word, segment and blend as above. Follow up by clapping, tapping, jumping, feeling (jaw dropping), and humming to further clarify the syllables in names.

Binding Rings

The metal rings used to bind paper can be used just like the other models to demonstrate segmenting and blending. Link them together to illustrate syllables or phonemes blended in a name, then unlink one by one to practice segmenting. They're great for students to use for guided practice or in centers, since they can be purchased in inexpensive larger lots. School district warehouses often stock them!

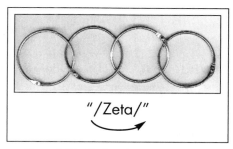

Figure 1.22 *Binding rings*

Zipper Pulls

Plastic zipper storage bags are cheap and easy to find. The ones with the rectangle zipper slides make great manipulatives for segmenting and blending (unzip to segment, zip sealed to blend) and identifying where sounds are located in words. When the bag is zipped closed, turn it so the slide is on the right side as you model in front of students (so they see the slide move from left to right). Move it to the left, unzipping, as you segment each syllable or phoneme in a name. Turn the open bag around again, so the slide is back on the right side and move it continuously to the left as you blend the sounds back together (resealing the bag). When students use the bags themselves, the slide should always be on their left to begin, so it moves from left to right as letters in words do (see Figure 1.23).

Use the zippers to reinforce the concepts of beginning (or first), middle, ending (or last) sound: "Show me on your model where you hear the /t/ sound in Elliot's name. Repeat: *Elliot.*" Students move the zipper, voicing the sounds in the word, then stopping the slide where they identify the target sound (in this example, at the end, as shown in Figure 1.24). Alternatively, say two names, like *Jenice* and *Donald,* asking students to move the slide to the position in the words where they hear the matching sound (in this case, the middle, as shown in Figure 1.25).

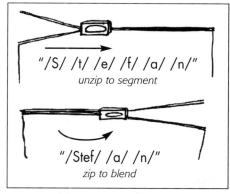

Figure 1.23 *Zipper storage bags*

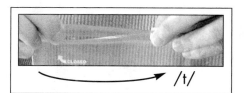

Figure 1.24 *"I hear /t/ at the end of Elliot!"*

Figure 1.25 *"I hear /n/ in the middle of Jenice and Donald!"*

Cardstock and Index Cards

I use cardstock two ways. First, a full 8½ x 11 sheet represents a whole word, then I cut off sections, one at a time (thirds for three phonemes, fourths for four phonemes, etc.), as we listen inside the word for sounds. (What a great visual: using scissors to literally chop a whole into its parts, as shown in Figure 1.26). I slide the pieces back together to represent blending and pull them apart again to segment. The possibilities for phoneme manipulation using cardstock are endless. For example, cut off the first third to represent deleting the beginning phoneme. What word/sound remains? Put a different-color sheet behind the remaining two

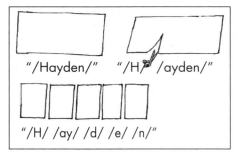

Figure 1.26 *Using cardstock pieces to represent beginning sounds and phonemes*

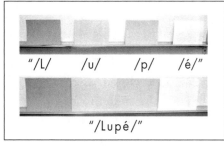

Figure 1.27 *Using cardstock pieces to represent phonemes*

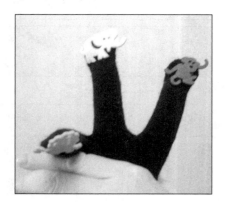

Figure 1.28 *Using index cards to represent syllables*

thirds to represent changing the initial phoneme. What word do you have now? The same can be done to focus on ending sounds. Cardstock pieces may be used to represent syllables and onset and rime, too. When modeling, manipulate the cardstock on your chalkboard tray or in a pocket chart.

Second, full sheets of cardstock nicely represent syllables or individual phonemes (use one whole sheet per phoneme, as shown in Figure 1.27). Again, slide them together on your chalkboard tray or in a pocket chart to represent blending; pull them apart to represent segmenting. Different colors can be used to depict beginning, middle, and ending sounds. Manipulate the pieces in all kinds of ways to play with phonemes (add, delete, or substitute sounds).

Index cards serve as smaller versions of the cardstock, thus making perfect manipulatives for guided practice or centers. Students move the pieces on their desks, on the floor, or at a table. They can cut them apart, as in the first example to the left, or use them whole, as shown second.

> ### *Fun Variations*
>
> *Do the same lessons on the overhead using colored transparencies. Just cut them into rectangles (which you can further cut apart) to fit your demonstrations.*

Get double duty from those colored plastic shapes made for overhead math lessons. Use the rectangles and squares (each square can represent a phoneme, for example) for another variation!

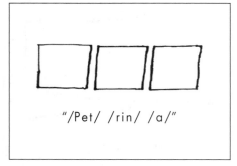

Figure 1.29 *The glove puppet shows three segmented phonemes, while voicing the initial sound (emphasized by wiggling and bending the first finger forward).*

The glove puppet shows four segmented phonemes.

Here, those four phonemes are blended (or "smushed") back together again.

Glove Puppets

You can manipulate sounds in names with as many as five phonemes with fun, easy-to-make glove puppets (see Figure 1.29). Using hot glue, apply foam shapes (found in craft stores) or pom-poms to the fingertips of cheap gloves. If a name or word has four phonemes, for instance, hold four fingers up, tightly together, to represent the whole word (for better control, wrap your other hand around your palm). Say the whole word, moving your fingers together in a wave or bow. Hold them upright again, then separate, bend and wiggle each individual finger from left to right (your right to left), voicing the sounds as they're segmented. Keep them separated to indicate the distinct phonemes. Next, bend them forward and together in turn to demonstrate blending! Wave or bow the fingers together as you voice the whole word again. It's a word bow! Thank you! Thank you!

Following your model, students can practice with their hands, using each finger to represent a syllable or phoneme. You might also make enough glove puppets to use with small groups.

Clay

Elongate a small block of clay as you voice the sounds in a name. Smush it back into a block to blend. Stretch it again, and cut off pieces to represent syllables or phonemes. Stick them back together to blend.

Models Are Versatile

Be creative in how you use the models. They're highly adaptable, since they can be put together and taken apart in varied ways. Review how the elastics, pipe cleaners with beads, and Unifix models were used for syllables and onset and rime as well as phonemes. Likewise, you can extend your use of any of these models for teaching and practicing:

- words in sentences
- syllables
- onsets and rimes
- rhyming
- beginning sounds
- ending sounds
- middle sounds
- substituting sounds
- adding sounds
- deleting sounds

"Oh,   lovely   mud!"

"Oh, lovely mud!"

Figure 1.30 *Here's "Kid Smush" showing segmenting and blending words in a sentence.*

You'll see I use these same concrete models over and over in many of the lessons throughout this book. They add an extra level of visual clarity for all students and provide extra support for those who are still developing their understanding of these underlying concepts even as we are working with letter sounds. In short, they make the lessons more effective for everyone!

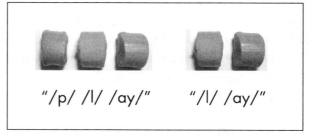

"/p/ /l/ /ay/"   "/l/ /ay/"

Figure 1.31 *This is another example using the clay model, this time to practice deleting sounds: "Starting with the word play, take off the beginning sound. What word do you have now?"*

CHAPTER 2

More Ideas for Teaching Phonological Awareness With the Name Wall

Ongoing work with the concrete models from Chapter 1 will radically improve your students' understanding of how sounds work in words. Here are several other learning experiences with names designed to further build their phonological awareness capabilities.

Important Points Pertaining to All Lessons

As you study the lessons, consider these important points:

- Always start by modeling. Model, model, model while thinking aloud about what you're doing. Follow with guided practice. Demonstrations and guidance are paramount to success before moving to independent practice. Follow the "I Do, We Do, You Do" approach.

- Be explicit regarding the purpose for lessons and practice sessions. Notice how my dialogued examples always include this important element. Students need to understand why their doing what they're doing. Debrief about the hows and whys as you conclude experiences.

- The lessons are meant to be repeated. Many students need multiple experiences with these processes in order for sufficient growth to occur.

- Over time, extend the lessons beyond students' names to involve other words. The procedures remain exactly the same.

Phonological Awareness Activities

Photo Fun!

To prepare for the following lessons, take one each of the small, wallet-size school pictures you get at the beginning of the year and glue them to one sheet of paper so that each student is represented. Make an overhead transparency, cut them out, and you have a class set of overhead pictures! Or, once you've taken individual pictures with a digital camera, insert each student's photo into a single-page Word document, right-click to "format picture" and resize with the moving arrows. Then, print the photos on a transparency. (Naturally, if your classroom is equipped with a document camera, this step isn't necessary). Also, make a photocopy of the master for each student so they can cut them out to make individual sets. Give everyone a manila envelope with a brad closure to store their copies. True, the initial preparation of the masters takes time. But, it's really worth it! We use the photo sets for all kinds of innovative activities and as manipulatives in centers.

Overhead Sorting With Students' Photos

Demonstrate how to sort names by beginning, ending, or vowel sounds using your set of overhead photos. Place some photos on the overhead, representing just a few sounds. The example below shows a beginning lesson in kindergarten, so I'm using five names as we focus on initial sounds: *Felicia, Lily, Sebastian, Fritz,* and *Sammi.* Remember, young learners' first experiences are more successful if we use names with continuous sounds (as opposed to stop sounds like /p/, /b/, and /t/) and work with only a few different sounds at once. Adapt the lesson to compare only two initial sounds to make it easier. As students' abilities grow, compare more photos and sounds at once.

As readers and writers we have to be able to listen inside words for sounds. Here's a fun way to practice! Let's place a few of our classmates' pictures on the overhead and sort them for beginning sounds. When we sort, we have to say the names slowly and stretch those beginning sounds to clearly hear and feel them. [*I like to demonstrate this using the elastic models or mini-slinky.*] Watch me. /Fffff/ /elicia/, /fffff/ /elicia/. I can feel and hear how Felicia's name starts with /fffff/. See how I'm putting the brakes on after that first sound in Felicia's name?

Do it with me. Feel how your top teeth are touching your bottom lip. [*I provide mirrors for students to see their mouth positions.*] Also, you can feel a slight stream of air come downward out of your mouth as you say /fffff/. Put your hand to your mouth and feel that as you stretch the beginning sound in Felicia's name /fffff/. Now, looking at our friends' pictures on the overhead, whose name also begins with the sound /fffff/? Let me test each person's name by stretching out those beginning sounds. Let's see, /Lllll/ /ily/. Nope, *Lily* starts with /lllll/; my mouth is open a bit when I make that sound, not closed with my teeth touching my lip like with /fffff/. /Sssss/ /ebastian/. Nope, *Sebastian* starts with /sssss/; my lips are apart and my teeth are together as I make that sound, /sssss/. /Fffff//ritz/, /fffff/ /ritz/. Now I hear the same

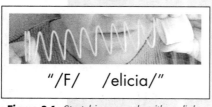

"/F/   /elicia/"

Figure 2.1 *Stretching sounds with a slinky*

beginning sound. And, if I check my mouth position, I can see and feel it's the same as when I say /Fffff//elicia/ [*modeling using the mirror as a visual and placing my hand to my mouth to feel the stream of air*]. Yep, /Fffff/ /ritz/ and /Fffff/ /elicia/ start with the same sound so I will move them into their own column to sort them together on the overhead. This last photo is of /Sssss/ /ammi/. No, /Sssss/ /ammi's/ name doesn't start with /fffff/. So, we have /Fffff/ /elicia/ and /Fffff/ /ritz/ sorted together. Let's sort the other names. /Lllll/ /ily/. [*I continue to demonstrate with the slinky model.*]

The lesson continues as the students and I work together to:

- orally stretch and exaggerate the sounds
- use a concrete model (such as the slinky) to visually demonstrate what we're doing
- feel and characterize how the sounds are made in our mouths
- check how our mouths look in a mirror
- compare one sound to another

Once you've sorted all the photos, a great way to extend the activity (especially if you don't have any other student names with the target sounds) is to place small objects to sort on the overhead. My kids love it when we use little plastic animals (the kind that come in packages of 20 or so found in the toy section of dollar stores). For this lesson, we could continue to test and sort a lion, snake, swan, frog, and fish; see Figure 2.2.

Figure 2.2 *Overhead sorting with student photos and concrete objects*

Provide guided practice next. Remove the photos and objects from the overhead. Have students find their copies of Felicia, Lily, Sebastian, Fritz and Sammi's photos from their sets. They re-sort them on their desks, while you provide guidance on the overhead. Then they orally volunteer other names or words that fit the sort, pointing out where they belong. If appropriate, have children mix up the photos once more and re-sort them on their own, checking with a partner. Remind them how important it is to say the names as they test and sort. You might also move the photos and plastic animals to a center, where students can re-sort independently or with a buddy. Strugglers can take a copy of the photos home to sort again under a parent's guidance. (I always have extra copies of the photo master on hand for this purpose.) They might also be asked to find objects that fit the sort at home.

After the guided practice, debrief:

How does sorting names by sounds help us? We have to be able to hear how sounds match from word to word, so we can use the names on our Wall to help us when we're stuck. Plus, we have to be able to hear the sounds in words to write and blend sounds in words to read. Remember when we used the pipe cleaners and beads and the Unifix cubes to help us see and hear sounds in classmates' names? This is another way to practice. Activities like this give us the know-how to work with sounds in words.

These ideas reach another level of clarity starting in Chapter 3, when you show students how to tie sounds together with letters using the Name Wall.

As students gain facility with beginning sounds, follow the same procedure when teaching them to differentiate ending sounds, then vowel sounds. Naturally, if your students don't need work in the area of beginning sounds, start by sorting photos for ending sounds. Refer to the developmental guidelines for phonemic awareness in your state grade-level standards and keep up on your informal and formal assessments. Knowing where your students are and how they're progressing will guide your instruction.

Differentiated Practice With Students' Photos

Once you adapt the lesson above to provide modeling and guided experiences sorting sounds in names, here are some ideas for meeting diverse needs as you provide further practice. Note how they involve partners or group work, forcing students to be more verbal (which is what we want during phonemic awareness exercises).

- More-able students work with a buddy to sort *all* the photos in their class set for beginning, ending, or vowel sounds in congruence with their needs. In later first grade and beyond, students might fold paper to make columns to record the names as they are sorted (they may use the Name Wall to aid spelling). If this is too difficult or too time consuming, have them work with half, a third, or a fourth of the photos.

- On-level students may be asked to work with a partner to re-sort the classmates you sorted together on the overhead. You may have them include a few other classmates' photos, representing one or two additional sounds not covered in the shared lesson.

- Struggling students may be asked to meet with you or with a tutor, volunteer, or aide (ideally one who observed the initial lesson) in a small group to re-sort the pictures from the shared overhead work. Under your guidance, individuals should use the concrete models to stretch the sounds and check their mouth positions in mirrors to reinforce learning.

Sound Boards With Names

Sound boards (Wagstaff, 2001) enable you to teach and practice phonological awareness with fun, game-like activities students love! To prepare the "board" (which is really just a sheet of paper), you'll use a copy of the master of students' pictures you prepared for name sorting on the overhead. Choose four students to represent the top of four columns on the board, then make enough copies for the entire class. Use your knowledge of developmental phonological awareness principles and your students' achievement levels to determine where to start. For this example, I'll use more complex, multisyllabic names along with simpler ones to demonstrate how to make the activity multi-level. Additionally, I'll model and provide guided practice in listening for ending sounds, which is more difficult than matching beginning sounds, but easier than vowel sounds.

To get started, disperse the sound boards and explain the purpose of the game you're about to play.

Today, we'll be working with some of our friends from the Name Wall to once again hear and identify the sounds making up their names. Remember, this will help us as we work to hear sounds in words to write them and sound out words to read them. Don't worry if your picture is not on *this* sound board. Everyone will have a chance to be represented as we practice with different sound boards over time.

[*I pass out some type of marker students can use to match sounds on their boards. You might use bingo chips, dried beans, or something edible (no clean up!).*]

Figure 2.3 *Sound board*

Here are some Cheerios. We'll use them to mark our matches on the board. Don't eat any until I tell you to do so. Now, look at the top of your sound board. Here we have *Shelly, Meg, Kevin,* and *Joseph.* Let's stretch each person's name to hear the sounds they're made of [*I use a glove puppet to concretely demonstrate*]: /shshshshsh/ /eeeee/ /lllll/ /yyyyy/, /mmmmm/ /eeeee/ /ggggg/, /kkkkk/ /eeeee/ /vvvvv/ /iiiii/ /nnnnn/, and /jjjjj/ /ooooo/ /sssss/ /eeeee/ /fffff/. Let's start by making sure you can smush those sounds back together to make their names. Ready? I'll say the individual sounds and you put a Cheerio on the name that matches. /Mmmmm/ /eeeee/ /ggggg/. Listen again. /Mmmmm/ /eeeee/ /ggggg/. Where did you make the match? Yes, Meg's name is made up of the sounds /mmmmm/ /eeeee/ /ggggg/. Repeat that with me. /Mmmmm/ /eeeee/ /ggggg/, Meg. Great! Let's try another. /Jjjjj/ /ooooo/ /sssss/ /eeeee/ /fffff/.

[*Proceed in the same fashion to match the other three names. When using edibles, I like to say, "You may eat the markers on your board now before we go on to something new."*]

Now that we've listened inside each name for its sounds, let's work on matching ending sounds with the friends on our board. If we can hear the connections between the names on our Name Wall and words we are trying to read and write, we can use the names to help us when we are stuck. Before we begin, let's listen inside the names once more to hear each ending sound. [*I use a zipper pull or glove puppet to visually demonstrate ending sound or last sound.*] First we have /shell/ /yyyyy/. What's that ending sound? /Yyyyy/. [*If appropriate, I model and discuss mouth positions with these sounds to give students another clue to help make matches on the sound board.*] In the next column there's /me/ /ggggg/. [*And so on.*]

Now let's match some together. Which name has the same ending sound as the word *fountai nnnnn*? Test the names on your board. Let's see, /Shell/ /yyyyy/, /fountai/ /nnnnn/. No, those don't match. They don't sound or feel the same at the end. /Me/ /ggggg/, /fountai/ /nnnnn/. No, those don't match either. /Kevi/ /nnnnn/, /fountai/ /nnnnn/. Yep, I hear /nnnnn/ at the end of each of those words. I also notice my mouth is in the same position for both. My tongue is tapping the top of my mouth just behind my teeth as I voice /nnnnn/. It feels the same at the end of /Kevi/ /nnnnn/ and /fountai/ /nnnnn/. Yes, I hear and feel the match. Do you? Try it with me. Let's show the match by putting a Cheerio in the column with Kevin's picture. So, if I was writing about the time I played in a /fountai/ /nnnnn/ and I was stuck on that ending sound, I could use the name /Kevi/ /nnnnn/ to help me. See? That's why it's important to be able to hear and make connections to our Name Wall. Let's try another.

Continue guided practice, matching words together. Over time, after work with several sound boards and lots of student success, withdraw some of the support. For example, on the other end of the support continuum, simply say, "Match the sound at the end of *cookie*. Test your board by saying the names aloud to yourself." After wait-time, "Now check with a partner. How did you do? Where did you make the match? Why?"

Differentiated Practice With Sound Boards

The difficulty of any sound board depends on whether students are listening for larger units of sound (i.e., syllables, rimes=easier) or smaller units of sound (phonemes=harder), the position of the sounds within the words, the complexity of the names of students pictured in the columns, the number of students pictured (or the number of columns to compare for matches), and the type of words offered to test and match. Single-syllable names and words where continuous sounds are being matched are easiest, while a mix of simple and multisyllabic words with stop sounds to match makes the activity multilevel.

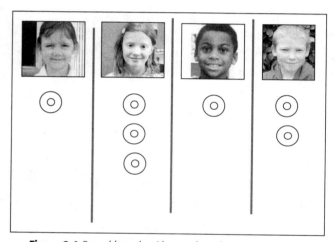

Figure 2.4 *Sound boards with cereal markers*

- Your most advanced students can work individually or with partners to hunt for matches to *write* in the columns. With this lesson, students would look for words ending in /e/, /g/, /n/, and /f/. Of course, since letters are now involved, you're integrating phonemic awareness practice with phonics.

- Your on-level students might also record matches in the columns using a word bank (or list of words) as a guide. Or, they could do the same using word cards in a center.

- *Even easier*: Have students use concrete objects or picture cards to match. Each time they find a match, they write the corresponding letter or letter combination in the correct column. So, if a kinder-gartner finds a picture of an egg, he or she writes a *g* in the Meg column. Great letter formation practice! (See Figure 2.5.)

Figure 2.5 *Sound boards with picture cards*

- Students who struggle benefit from having more time to practice testing and matching words orally. They also benefit by having fewer sounds to discriminate between. You or another qualified individual can lead them in a small-group setting, providing them with essential guidance and immediate feedback. Use the same sound board as you used for your modeled and guided lesson with cereal for markers. But this time, take the sound board and fold a column under. Now, students have three names to work with. If this is still too difficult, fold back another column (see Figure 2.6). Voilà! Instant differentiation!

- As described with the overhead-picture-sorting activity, strugglers should be given the opportunity to use mirrors to check how a sound looks and feels and to use assorted concrete models as they stretch words and identify individual sounds.

One of the great characteristics of sound boards is that they are so versatile! You can use them to help students practice the number of syllables in words, rhyming words, beginning sounds, ending sounds, medial sounds, complex onsets (with consonant blends), rimes (chunks), or the number of sounds in words. As you work with the boards as shown in the lesson, students are building their abilities to identify, match, discriminate, segment, and blend sounds! And, as the differentiation ideas indicate, it's easy to integrate phonics with the boards, too!

For more detailed information on using sound boards, ready-made boards to go along with favorite children's books, and set-to-go directions for aides, tutors, or volunteers to use as they work with students, see my book *Irresistible Sound-Matching Sheets and Lessons That Build Phonemic Awareness* (Scholastic, 2001). This resource is a great time-saver!

Thumbs Up, Thumbs Down

Thumbs Up, Thumbs Down is another way to practice matching sounds. It's ideal for transition times, since no materials are needed. I'll focus this example on connecting vowel sounds in names. As with the other lessons, this procedure is adaptable for practicing all kinds of sound matching: onsets, rimes, beginning and ending sounds, and so on.

> **Note**
>
> *Do a mini-lesson for students who are ready to investigate cases where the sound matches but the spelling differs. Joseph's name is a perfect example of this. Explain though Joseph ends in the spelling p-h for the /f/ sound, most words ending in /f/ will be spelled with the letter f. As students hunt for matches to record, they'll see how this works. Have them star or highlight any p-h words they find. Great phonics practice!*

> **Hint**
>
> *Don't have concrete objects or picture cards? Look for plastic mini toys packaged in lots at dollar stores and use small magazine pictures instead. Better yet, show students what you're looking for and have them bring in examples from home to use in your centers.*

Figure 2.7 *Folded sound board*

As we're lining up to go to music, let's play Thumbs Up, Thumbs Down. This time, let's practice listening to hear the connections between vowels. Say Enrique's name with me. [*Enrique.*]

Now, let's segment his name into syllables. Here's his name coming out of my mouth so you can see it. [*As I say it, I bring six linked Unifix cubes (two per syllable) to my mouth, then "pull" them out, showing them in my fingers.*] /Enrique/. I'll break his name into syllables. Watch and listen. [*As each syllable is pronounced, I break away two Unifix cubes*]: /En/ /ri/ /que/. Now, say the syllables with me [*I point to the pairs of cubes as we say the syllables together*].

[*Next, I link the cubes back together.*] Blend the syllables back together and we have /Enrique/. [*If students need more support distinguishing syllables, use the clapping, feeling, or humming syllable detection methods listed on page 23.*]

Let's take the first syllable in Enrique's name [*breaking the cubes apart into syllables again*]: /En/. What's the vowel sound in /En/? Let's stretch the sounds [*I break the two linked cubes into individuals*]: /Eeeee/ /nnnnn/. What do you hear? How does that vowel sound feel in your mouth? That's the sound we are going to match for this round of Thumbs Up, Thumbs Down.

[*After feeling and characterizing the sound, I give students names and words to match, showing thumbs up for a positive match, and thumbs down when sounds don't match.*]

Here's your first word: *Meg*. Remember to say it, stretching the sounds. Does it match? Thumbs up, thumbs down. [*Students show thumbs up.*] Yes! Thumbs up! The vowel in /M/ /eeeee/ /g/ sounds and feels the same as the vowel in the first syllable of /Eeeeen/ rique. Repeat both names with me, emphasizing those vowels and watch your neighbor's mouth to see that they look the same. Ready?

/M/ /eeee/ /g/. /Eeeeen/ rique. See it? Feel it? Here's another name to match with the first vowel sound in *Enrique*. *Seth*. Repeat it. Thumbs up, thumbs down.

Be sure to include thumbs-down examples and talk through the matches or non-matches as students respond. If they experience trouble, incorporate a concrete model.

Again, matching shorter, one syllable names and words is easier than longer, multisyllabic names and words. Yes, the first vowel sound in *Enrique* matches the last vowel sound in *Mohamed*, but the process of confirming that match is much more complex than the examples above. Keep this in mind as you work with your students.

As you involve students in lots of phonological awareness practice over time, you'll see a difference in their Thumbs Up, Thumbs Down responses. At first, and this has never failed to be true in my classrooms, students will be unsure of themselves, changing their responses as they look at their neighbors, unable to confidently distinguish and match sounds. Later, though, their abilities bolstered by our repeated efforts, they'll respond more quickly and accurately.

Management Tip

To increase students' accountability for their own responses, pose the question, then give them think-time. I count quietly to five. On five, the kids show their signal against their chests.

Match a Sound

This is a more open activity, where students are free to make matches to sounds anywhere in one another's names. The idea is to get them practicing listening for varied connections. Make activity mats by cutting a large picture of a single object into sections, one for each phoneme. The apple at the top of the mat at right is broken into three parts for three phonemes /a/, /p/, and /l/. Each phoneme creates a column. Students take their classmate photo set, say and stretch each name, listening for connections to the sounds inside the pictured word. With the apple activity mat, they listen for /a/, /p/, and /l/ anywhere inside the names. When a connection is made, the photo is placed in the appropriate column. For *apple*, then, we place photos of Ms. Wag, Manuel, Fabrice, and Tanner in the first column because they all have /a/ somewhere inside them. Esperanza's photo goes in the middle for /p/, and Lily, Shelly, Akeelah, Charlie, Lucio, and Danielle's photos go in the final /l/ column.

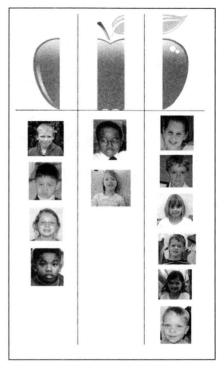

Figure 2.7 *Apple activity mat*

Beginning, Middle, End

As the name suggests, in this activity, students identify where they hear a connection across names and words—at the beginning, middle, or end. Simply point to a photo on your Name Wall and say another name or word that shares a sound connection. After everybody has think-time, students hold an arm straight out with a closed fist. To identify where they hear a match, they touch their shoulder (the beginning of their arm), their elbow (the middle of their arm), or their fist (the end of their arm). Pointing to Cathy's photo on the Wall, I say *Imonee*. Students touch their fists to indicate the match is at the end. Pointing to *Jarred*, I say *stirring*. They touch their elbows to indicate the match in the middle.

Name War

Name War is played like the classic card game War. Each partner flips over a student photo from their "deck" (their set of class photos) to see if there's a sound match. The match can occur in any position. (For instance, *Sri* and *Tessa* make a match since they share /s/, though it's in different spots within the names.) When there's a match, the first player to identify it grabs the two photos. If there is no connection, the two photos stay down and the next photos are flipped on top until a match is won. The great thing about this game is that it gets the players segmenting names to find matching sounds and talking about what they find as they confirm or disconfirm connections.

Name Spin

For this activity, you'll need number spinners and class photo sets. Working alone, in pairs, or in small groups, students spread out a set of photos face up and take turns spinning for a number. With each spin, players try to find a name with that number of syllables or phonemes to "win" a photo. For example, Whitney's photo is won on the number five since it has five phonemes. To keep the photo, students must segment the name to demonstrate that it matches the spinner. The same activity can be done with dice in place of spinners.

Photo Clap

Students pick one photo at a time from their class set, clapping the syllables in the names. They can also clap the beginning sound, then the rest of the name, or clap all the phonemes.

> **Variation**
>
> *Students sort the photos as they clap: by number of syllables or by number of phonemes.*

Match the Models

Students match photos of their classmates to varied concrete models by segmenting names into phonemes or syllables. Once a match is made, they segment and blend the name using the model.

> **Management Hint**
>
> *If students are "Photo Clapping" in a center, have them wear garden gloves for noise control.*

For example, Mari's photo is matched with a pipe cleaner and bead model representing three phonemes; Ahmaad's photo is paired with an elastic model representing four phonemes; Ty's photo is matched with a Unifix model showing two phonemes, and Adrianna's photo is matched with linked binding rings representing four syllables; see Figure 2.8.

Figure 2.8 *Match the Models*

Roll Call

Practice substituting sounds with this catchy chant. The silly name variations you create will make your students giggle! You'll find this perfect for morning circle time in kindergarten or morning meeting in first grade. It also makes a fun transition activity.

Say the chant with a target sound to substitute for the beginning sound in classmates names. Here, the target sound is /ch/.

Let's say our names with /ch/ today
Let's say our names with /ch/ today
Let's say our names with /ch/ today
Just for fun.

Proceed around the circle (or around tables or down rows) reinventing names as you go. So, *Joey* becomes *Choey*, *Natalie* becomes *Chatalie*, *Santos* becomes *Chantos*, and so on. It's also fun to have a volunteer point to photos on the Name Wall to lead the class in this sound substitution activity. Once students are adept at substituting beginning sounds, have them substitute ending sounds.

Spin-offs From Roll Call

1. A student photo is placed at the top of a pocket chart.
2. Students use the beginning sound in the name at the top to substitute for the beginning sound in their classmates' pictures.
3. As each "new" name is voiced, the picture is placed in the pocket chart.
4. When all the photos are placed, the chart is "reread" as fast as possible.
5. Change the photo at the top and go again!

Complete the activity in a shared setting first, then use it as a center or for partner work. When students are ready, have them substitute ending sounds to match the name at the top of the pocket chart.

For more of a challenge, place two, three, or four students' photos with varying beginning sounds at the top of the chart to create columns. Students choose which beginning sound to substitute in a name, voice the "new" name, then place the photo in the appropriate column. Once all photos are sorted, they reread the whole chart of funny names going down the columns as quickly as possible! You might time the reread with a stopwatch. This motivates students to read the chart again to try to improve their time.

Three Favorite Phonemic Awareness Name Songs

The power of rhythm in aiding learning cannot be overstated. In chants like Roll Call, not only does learning become fun, but the melodies get stuck in students' heads. I hear them singing them on the playground and often, on my ride home from school, they're playing in my head, too! Below are three of my other favorites. Try innovating on familiar tunes to compose your own.

Our Names Go Marching
Sung to the tune: "The Ants Go Marching"

Who's name has <u>three</u> sounds in it? Hoorah! Hoorah!

Who's name has <u>three</u> sounds in it? Hoorah! Hoorah!

<u>Mary's</u> name has <u>three</u> sounds in it! /M/ /ar/ /y/

And they all blend together <u>/M/ /ar/ /y/ Mary!</u>

Change the underlined parts to sing names with any number of phonemes! For really long names, just sing the name in syllables or as a whole on the last line of the song:

Who's name has <u>seven</u> sounds in it? Hoorah! Hoorah!

Who's name has <u>seven</u> sounds in it? Hoorah! Hoorah!

<u>Samantha's</u> name has <u>seven</u> sounds in it! <u>/S/ /a/ /m/ /a/ /n/ /th/ /a/</u>

And they all blend together <u>/Sa/ /man/ /tha/</u>!

Tie in the Name Wall by having a volunteer use a pointer to point to the photo and name as it's sung.

If You Think You Know This Friend
Sung to the tune of: "If You're Happy and You Know It"

If you think you know this friend, shout it out!

If you think you know this friend, shout it out!

If you think you know this friend, can you tell me who it is?

If you think you know this friend, shout it out!

1. Sing a verse.
2. Give students clues to the name you have in mind from the ABC Name Wall. (You may give just one clue, or many. In the example below, I give two clues.)
3. A volunteer can come forward to point to the name once it's identified.
4. Sing the verse again, shouting out the name after each "shout it out!"

Example: After singing the verse I give the first clue: "This name has two syllables." We entertain which name it could be, testing responses by clapping, feeling or humming the syllables. Then, I give another clue: "This name has two syllables and the first one rhymes with the word *ten*." Students: "Kenya!" We repeat the song with Kenya's name:

If you think you know this friend, shout it out! Ken-ya!

If you think you know this friend, shout it out! Ken-ya!

If you think you know this friend, can you tell me who it is?

If you think you know this friend, shout it out! Ken-ya!

Sing the Sounds
My students love this tune, adapted from *I Like the Rain* (Belanger, 1988). Use it to isolate beginning or ending sounds in names:

We know Fabrice
We know Fabrice
How does it start?
/f/ /f/ /f/ /f/
We know Fabrice!

We know Shaday
We know Shaday
How does it start?
/sh/ /sh/ /sh/ /sh/
We know Shaday!

We know Chez
We know Chez
How does it start?
/ch/ /ch/ /ch/ /ch/
We know Chez!

To highlight ending sounds:

We know Chez
We know Chez
How does it end?
/z/ /z/ /z/ /z/
We know Chez!

You'll see another variation for singing chunks in Chapter 5.

Time-Saver

Whenever you sing or chant, stretch the learning by simply recording your students. They are very motivated to listen again to hear their voices on tape. Plus, the recording can be used in a center or for take-home activities.

Closing Thought

The use of phonological awareness activities should not be hit and miss. Work toward independence with grade-level goals.★ Of course, this can only happen with an appropriate amount of support and practice. Strugglers need more. Take Renee and Alberto. When teachers encounter students who can't segment words into sounds, they typically end up doing the work for them. "Listen, Renee, /Sssss/ /anta/. Hear it? *Santa* begins with /sssss/." Or, "Alberto, the first sound you hear in *bed* is /b/. /B/ /ed/. /B/!" While modeling is one way to help, it can't be the only solution or students never develop independence. The bottom line is that students have to meet grade-level standards themselves in order to successfully work through the stages of decoding and spelling. And, teachers have to know how to get them there. The ideas in Chapters 1 and 2 will boost your repertoire of strategies to make that happen.

★ *What is expected at different grade levels?*
   Every state now has phonological awareness goals included in their grade-level standards. If you don't have access to your state's document, search online for your state's office of education, then look under language arts standards, then phonemic awareness. The guidelines are similar from state to state, since they are based on research. The DIBELS benchmarks can also guide you (see http://dibels.uoregon.edu/) as can the scope and sequence for phonemic awareness within your school's adopted reading program.

CHAPTER 3

The ABC Name Wall for Letter-Sound Knowledge

It is a brand new school year, and first grader Lily recently went camping with her family. She is writing a story about her experience. She says, "I want to write, *I like to camp*. How do you write *camp*?" Peering over her paper, I see she has the words *I, like,* and *to*.

"How did you know how to write *I like to*?" I ask, while tracking and reading her paper.

"From the chart we made."

Sure enough, earlier in the week, we had shared the pen, using interactive writing (McCarrier, Fountas, & Pinnell, 1999) to record several sentences about our likes and dislikes as part of a back-to-school get-to-know-you activity.

"You're very smart to use something we've written to help you write your own story. Let me show you something else smart writers do. See our Name Wall? Whose name on the Wall starts with the same sound as the word *camp*?"

"*Catalina*?"

"Yes! So you need the letter c for the beginning sound in *camp*. Can you hear any other sounds inside the word *camp*?"

"/Mmmmm/?"

"Wow! That's a sound toward the end of the word *camp*. Is there a name on our Wall with the /mmmmm/ sound?"

"I'm not sure."

"Let me help you. I see the names /Lllll/ /ayla/ and /Mmmm/ /ulheem/. Which one has the /mmmmm/ sound?"

"*Mulheem*!"

"You're right! So, you need the letter *m* like in *Mulheem* for the /mmmmm/ sound in *camp*. Do you hear another sound there at the end?"

"/Ppppp/."

"Whose name on our Wall will help with /ppppp/?"

"Patrick!"

"You've got it! You've come up with a very good spelling for *camp* by connecting the sounds you hear to the spelling of names on our Wall. That's exactly why we have the Name Wall—to help us read and write new words! Keep listening for the sounds you hear in the words you're writing and connecting them to names on our Wall! This will make spelling them easier for you!"

This classroom scenario demonstrates the common-sense way the ABC Name Wall enables children to connect sounds and letters. Using classmate's names is a kid-friendly way to diminish confusion about those arbitrary squiggles and their abstract sounds. The goal of using names for phonological awareness (as shown in Chapters 1 and 2) is to heighten students' abilities to use these connections.

Phonological awareness and work with letter sounds go hand-in-hand. As we aim to build students' abilities to hear, manipulate, and understand sounds in words, we naturally want to show them how those sounds are represented in print. In other words, when working with sounds, we're compelled to extend those lessons to include letters. Best practice dictates we further push to include application. Using letter sounds in reading and writing should always be the overall goal. Lily's interaction with the ABC Name Wall shows how this is possible.

A caution here: Though it is true that phonemic awareness and letter-sound association are intertwined, we must attend closely to the progress of our students. Children who struggle to learn letter sounds may lack the understanding of what those letters are supposed to represent. When I encounter students who don't seem to be progressing with their peers, I always assess their phonemic awareness abilities (using DIBELS [2002], Adams [1998], or Blevins [2006], for example). This enables me to set up small groups to target those who need more intensive work with the phonemic awareness practice ideas in Chapters 1 and 2. Small-group work specific to the needs of those falling behind is critical to their overall success as readers and writers.

Say, for example, it was much later in the school year, and Lily was unable to articulate the sounds in the word *camp*. Because I know we've been immersed in phonological awareness practice and using our ABC Name Wall while reading and writing since the very beginning of the school year, this would send up a red flag. I'd immediately test her phonemic awareness abilities to pinpoint trouble spots and take action to accelerate her skills.

> ### Note
>
> *Be sure to review the Key Terms in the appendix if these ideas are new to you.*

Grade-Level Relevance

This chapter continues to cover curricular goals typical for kindergarten and first grade and beginning English language learners. We are merely extending our focus from Chapters 1 and 2 to include learning and using the alphabet. See "Building and Organizing the ABC Name Wall" and "Extending the ABC Name Wall" sections (pages 14–18) in Chapter 1 for logistical questions.

Pacing

I post names on the Wall all at once (see Chapter 1 for other options). I advocate incidental teacher modeling using multiple correspondences from the very start, and each week we highlight two (in kindergarten) to three (in first grade) letter-sound correspondences for intensive work. This way, in kindergarten, I can be sure I am thoroughly teaching letter names, letter formation, and letter sounds, while in first grade, I can be sure I'm thoroughly reviewing the same. Follow the same guidelines for English language learners. I highlight just two letter-sound correspondences if it is their first introduction to the alphabet (or if their skills are emergent), or three if I'm engaged in review or the students are more skilled (then, as noted below, I slowly increase the pace as appropriate). If you choose to post gradually and are not sure where to start, follow the scope and sequence of your adopted materials, extending your lessons to include work with names containing those same letter-sound correspondences.

Here's the weekly schedule I use for working with Names on the Wall:

Monday: Pick two (for kindergarten) or three (for first grade) letter-sound correspondences to highlight this week (slowly increase to four in first grade, if appropriate). Introduce the names and letter sounds (or reintroduce if they were already posted).

Tues.–Fri.: Practice these intensively throughout the week (See "Differentiated Practice Activities").

Friday: Post (or re-post) the names.

Use, use, use the names and letter sounds to read and write new words in multiple contexts for the rest of the school year! (See "Significant Lessons for Guided Spelling and Guided Decoding," Chapter 4.)

Introducing the ABC Name Wall to Build Letter-Sound Knowledge

Once you've introduced the Name Wall for phonological awareness as described in Chapter 1 (recall the examples using Mat and Becka's names on pages 19 and 22), also introduce the idea that the Wall will be used to learn and practice letters and letter-sound correspondences. You might begin by reviewing main points from your previous lessons, then launch into emphasis on using the sounds we hear to connect to *letters* in names.

> Our Name Wall is an important tool in our classroom. Besides helping us learn about sounds in words, we'll use it to help us learn how words and letters work. As we play with each other's names, we'll see how sounds and letters are important to us as readers and writers.

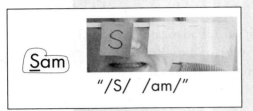

Figure 3.1 *Stretching Sam's name*

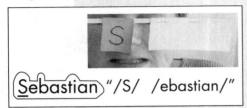

Figure 3.2 *Matching beginning sounds*

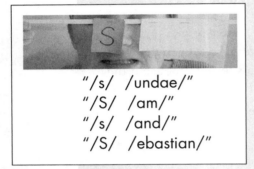

Figure 3.3 *Brainstorming /s/ words*

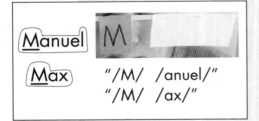

Figure 3.4 *Focusing on beginning sounds*

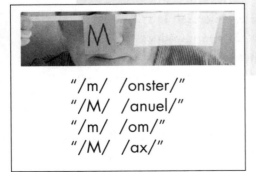

Figure 3.5 *Brainstorming /m/ words*

Remember using the pipe cleaners and beads and the Unifix cubes to pull apart and blend together those small, meaningless sounds in our names? As we become really good at hearing and working with the sounds, we'll be able to use the letters, too! Here's an example. If I say Sam's name slowly, stretching it out, I can hear the sounds it's made of . . . /Sssss/ /am/. [*I repeat segmenting and blending the onset and rime a few times with the elastic model.*] Those sounds have letters that represent them. Look at Sam's name card [*I take the card off the Name Wall and hold it up*] and you can see those letters. I want you to particularly notice the letter at the beginning of Sam's name. When you hear /sssss/ in words you're trying to write or see *s* in words you're reading, you can use Sam's name to help you remember the letter and sound until you know it by heart. You'll see, the names of all our classmates will be so useful to us!

Do we have any other friends' names on the Wall that start like /Sssss/ /am/ with the letter s? [*Students respond* Sebastian!]

[*I take Sebastian's name card off the Wall and hold it up.*] Yes, /Sssss/ /ebastian/ also starts with the letter *s*, since the first sound in his name is /sssss/ [*I demonstrate isolating the initial sound using the elastic model*]. Do you hear how *Sam* and *Sebastian* sound the same at the beginning? And, look at my mouth, my lips are apart just a bit . . . /Sssss/ /am/, /Ssssss/ /ebastian/. They sound and feel the same at the beginning and they both begin with the same letter, *s*.

If I'm writing about my delicious sundae, I hear and feel /sssss/ /undae/ starts with /sssss/. So, I use the letter *s* to spell it, just like at the beginning of *Sam* and *Sebastian*! Or, if I was writing about playing in the sand, I could also use their names to help me, since I hear /sssss/ again. Watch. [*I demonstrate isolating the beginning sound with the elastic model, then write the letter s on the first piece of cardstock and segment and blend repeatedly to overemphasize and visually demonstrate the connection.*] /Sssss/ /undae/, /Sssss/ /am/, /sssss/ /and/, /Sssss/ /ebastian/—they all start with the letter *s*! (See Figure 3.3.)

I repeat this demonstration using another pair of names that begin with the same letter, in this case *Max* and *Manuel* for the /m/ sound.

Before we continue with the guided practice portion of the lesson, let's debrief about the lesson so far: With beginning

English language learners, kindergartners, and beginning first graders, we emphasize initial letter-sound connections, since these are easier to hear and identify than the same phonemes at the end or middle of names. After all, the beginning sound is the most prominent feature in any name, and the ABC Name Wall is organized in alphabetical order to exploit that connection. However, as students develop proficiency with the beginning sounds on the Wall, we move on to using other phonemes within classmates' names. The process is the same no matter what part of a word is used to make an analogy: students have to first hear and understand the connection, then see how the letter(s) and letter-patterns are used across many words.

Note how for this introductory lesson, I focus on names with continuous sounds /s/ and /m/. Again, if you're not sure where to start, use your knowledge of your grade-level phonics scope and sequence to guide your work or consult your adopted reading program or state grade-level standards. In first grade, extend the lesson to work with three letter-sound correspondences. If you teach kindergarten and you're questioning introducing two letter sounds at once, see my article "Building Practical Knowledge of Letter-Sound Correspondences: A Beginner's Word Wall and Beyond." That year, I taught kindergarten just outside of Washington, D.C., and when we started the school year, not one child in a class of more than 20 knew one letter of their name! I found introducing two letters at one time was completely manageable for these children, even though they had minimal phonemic awareness and experience with letters. Keep in mind that one of the huge benefits of the Name Wall is that you'll continually be reviewing the letter sounds with those same names all year as you read and write, so there are multiple learning opportunities!

Guided Practice: Rainbow Writing

As your lesson continues, push for application of the concepts just demonstrated. Introductory lessons emphasize letter formation and phonemic awareness. Follow the next steps, working on one letter at a time: Model the uppercase and lowercase letter forms, as students record them on scratch paper. Then "rainbow write" (trace over the letters in different colors) while repeating the letter name and sound and voicing analogous words with the same initial sound (starting with your Name Wall names, of course!).

Explain, so students know why they're doing what they're doing:

> We need to practice s, the beginning letter in Sam and Sebastian's names, so we get to know it by heart and can use it to read and write new words. As we practice, let's repeat the letter name and the sound, then see who can give us a new word starting with that sound! We'll do it over and over as we change colors to rainbow write s.
>
> [Guide students so they have multiple repetitions of capital and lowercase s.]
>
> Wow! We sure came up with a lot of /sssss/ words. When writing those words then, we would need to start with the letter s just like we see at the beginning of Sam and Sebastian's names. If you need help remembering the sound for the letter s, use their photos on the Name Wall. If you can't remember how to form the letter s, again, look to the Wall for help. The names will be here all year to help you!

Figure 3.6 *Rainbow Writing*

Then move to *m*, following the same steps. Again, make a connection to reading and writing: "That's a lot of /mmmm/ words. See how Manuel and Max's names will help us read and write /mmmmm/ words?" Continue the routine for the third letter sound in first grade.

The goal of the next part of the lesson is to give students a cursory first look at how the names will help them decode beginning sounds in words.

> Let's look at a few words together, so you can see how we can use the letters in our names to read new words. Let's use the names we're focusing on this week: *Sam, Sebastian, Manuel, Max,* and *Felicia [the additional name is for the third letter-sound correspondence suggested for grade 1 and more-skilled English language learners].*

I write one simple word at a time on a Magna Doodle (this is a fun, motivating teaching tool!), then model using a name to help me decode. Writing *sat*, I say,

> I see this word looks the same at the beginning as Sam's name. So, the first sound is /sssss/ like /Sssss/ /am/. This word is /sssss/ /at/ [*I run my finger under the written word as I sound through it*], *sat*. [*Writing* man, *I say,*] I know /Mmmmm/ /anuel/'s name and see this word looks the same at the beginning, so it must start with the same sound /mmmmm/. This word is /mmmmm/ /an/. [*I run my finger under the word again as I sound through it*], *man*. In fact, the first beat in Manuel's name has that word in it! /Man/ /uel/! Here's another word [*I write it*]: *fun*. Since I know /Fffff/ /elicia/, I know this word starts with /fffff/. This word is /fffff/ /un/, *fun*. The more we get to know the names on our Name Wall, the more we can use those letters and sounds to read and write other words!

Beginning Each Week

To begin each week, pick another two or three letter sounds as targets, affixing the corresponding names to your center whiteboard with sticky tack. Modify the introductory lesson, but include these elements:

- emphasize the initial sound in each name
- isolate the sound while demonstrating with a concrete model
- connect the sound to the letter(s) while pointing to the Name Wall card
- identify other names with that correspondence, while isolating the beginning sound again using the elastic or Unifix model
- record the letter(s) representing the beginning sound on the model and demonstrate segmenting and blending with several other analogous words
- introduce the letter form, model uppercase and lowercase
- provide some type of guided practice, like rainbow writing, while repeatedly voicing the sound and generating analogous words so students experience application of the letter sounds

Another one of our favorites for introductory guided practice is to chant Roll Call (see page 40), substituting the target sounds of the week for the beginning sounds in our names. We try each sound for a name, then vote on our favorite variation. Everyone writes the uppercase and lowercase letter to record the results of each vote (this provides plenty of repeated letter formation practice!). Be sure to sum up the lesson with the overall purpose of the Wall, showing how you'll use the names to read and write lots of other words!

Throughout the Week: Differentiated Practice Activities

Throughout the week, we'll do many varied practice activities to build familiarity with the two or three featured letter-sound correspondences. This does not mean that every child will have mastery of each of these when the week is finished and the names are posted (or re-posted). However, with our continued use of the Name Wall in daily reading and writing, repetition is frequent and students' knowledge of letter names, letter forms, and letter sounds becomes solid over time. Three cheers for the support of the Name Wall!

Important Points Pertaining to All Activities

As you study the activities, consider these important points:

- Always start by modeling. Model, model, model while thinking aloud about what you're doing. Follow with guided practice before expecting students to do things on their own. Use the "I Do, We Do, You Do" plan whenever possible.

- Be explicit regarding the purpose of practice sessions. Students need to understand why they're doing what they're doing. Debrief about the hows and whys as you conclude experiences.

- The activities are meant to be repeated. Many students need multiple practice sessions for sufficient growth to occur.

- Over time, extend the activities beyond students' names to involve other words. The procedures remain exactly the same.

Practice Pages

Practice pages for the ABC Name Wall are designed to promote automaticity with letter names, letter forms, and letter sounds. Differentiated practice options also allow for work with the analogy strategies on varied levels.

I create a new Practice Page for the target letters each week. Here's how:

Figure 3.7 *Practice page*

1. While holding an 8½ x 11 sheet of paper vertically, fold under a three-inch column on the right side.

2. Mark the column with a bold, dotted, vertical line (this will indicate where students fold to hide the photos).

3. Glue the photos for the target letter sounds down the right column, evenly spaced.

4. Write the letters (uppercase and lowercase) for the beginning sounds and the students' first names in the left column. (*Note:* Digraphs are written with an uppercase first letter and lowercase second letter.)

Briefly explain the purpose of the Practice Page:

> As you know, we're working hard to learn the letter names, letter forms, and letter sounds of the alphabet, using our friends' names on the Name Wall. Practice Pages will help us review what we're learning. You'll get a new Practice Page every week to go along with the names we're studying. We'll keep the Pages in a folder, so we can reread them again and again, getting to know the letters and sounds by heart. This way, we can use what we know to make reading and writing easier!

Pass out the Page and read it together. Guide students to:

- point to the letter
- identify the letter name
- voice the sound
- read the student name
- point to the photo and repeat the student name

Next, assign these differentiated practice options based on student needs:

Figure 3.8 *Differentiated practice option A*

- Standard: Have students rainbow write over the letter and name. Taking a different-color crayon or marker each time, they trace the letter while saying the letter name and sound over and over again, until they have a rainbow of colors. They then rainbow write over the student's first name (reading the name while tracing).

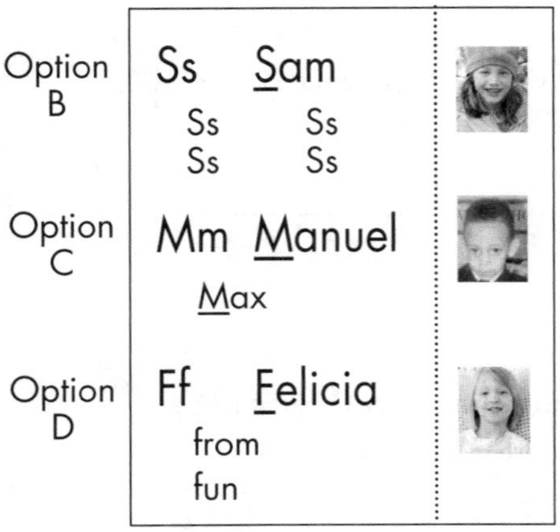

- Option A: *Example of rainbow writing.* Once finished, they move on to rainbow write the other beginning letters and names on the Practice Page. Finally, they fold the photo column under (hiding the picture clue), point, and read. The challenge here is: can they say the letter names and sounds and read the first names without turning the page to view the photo clues? (The photo clues are used as support if students get stuck, but they can also be used for self-checking.)

Figure 3.9 *Differentiated practice options*

- Option B (*More challenge*): *Rainbow writing plus freehand letter formation practice.* Students complete the steps above, then, in the space under each name, they write the uppercase and lowercase letters to practice letter formation. This is done with a pencil. (See Figure 3.9.)

- Option C (*Even more challenge*): Students complete Option A, then write analogous classmates' names from the Name Wall under the target letter. (See Figure 3.10.)

- Option D (*Still more challenge*): Students complete Option A, then add a few simple, single-syllable words beginning with the target letter sound.

Figure 3.10 *Differentiated practice option C*

Practice Pages can also be done with emphasis on the *ending* sounds in names.

When you have multiple names for one letter-sound correspondence, list the names and photos together (as in Figure 3.10) or feature different children on different weeks. In Kindergarten, you'll have extra space since the focus is on two sounds per week. If desired, include a "review" letter and name from a previous week at the bottom.

Practice Folders

My students keep two-pocket folders to store their accumulating Practice Pages. I'll give them just three or four minutes once or twice a week to reread from their folders. This builds automaticity with letter names and sounds. Remember, if they get stuck, they just turn the page and look at the photo clue. Support is built right in! You'll be amazed at how quickly students master letters and sounds using Practice Pages! Occasionally, you might also allow them to take their Practice Folders home to show off their learning.

Sound Boards

Feature student photos representing the week's target sounds at the top of your sound board. After working on hearing and matching beginning sounds orally (instructions on page 34), give students a word bank or word cards in a center, or have them hunt for words beginning with those sounds to *write* in the columns. Review the differentiated practice ideas on page 36.

Don't forget to use Sound Boards to practice final and medial letter sounds and chunks (you'll see how in Chapter 5) as your students' abilities grow!

Figure 3.11 *A student records analogous words for /sh/, Shauntelle; /j/, Jordan; and /k/, Kim.*

Numbered Heads Together Morning Message

I write a Morning Message to my students every morning. A few times each week, I provide specific practice with the target letters by leaving blanks in the message where these particular letter sounds belong. First, we read the message together, then I tell teams (my students are seated at tables and each student is assigned a number 1, 2, 3, 4, or 5 for their team) to put their heads together, using the names of the week to figure out which letter(s) goes in each blank (see Figure 3.12). I give them a few minutes to discuss. Then, I roll a die, calling the number that comes up. Each of these students stands to represent their team. I call on one volunteer to come forward and fill in the blank, sharing their team answer. Each is discussed and connected to the Name Wall names. As weeks go by, I include blanks for letter sounds we've focused on in previous weeks.

Note

Numbered Heads Together is a cooperative learning strategy (Kagan, Kagan, & Kagan, 2000).

Dear Cla___ ,

_riday is our _ield trip to the _arket. Don't _orget to bring _nack_!

Love,
_s. Wag.

Figure 3.12 *As students gain proficiency with letter sounds, leave blanks in the middle and at the end of words on a regular basis.*

Variation

After reading the message, volunteers circle the letters they recognize, connecting to names on the Wall. For example, Stefan says, "I see l (circling l) in love just like in Lucio's name!" After shared work, the message can become a center where students continue to circle letters they see, making multiple connections to the Name Wall. This is one of my favorite activities, since I can write something purposeful to engage students and review skills at the same time. We do this almost every day since it's quick and fun and gives us tons of review!

Read, Match, & Write

(Adapted from Pinnell & Fountas, 1998) Prepare a three-column master like the one below, labeling the first column "Read," the middle column "Match," and the third column, "Write." Place small name cards (36-point font) for the target sounds of the week in a box. Students pick a name, read it (using the Name Wall for help if necessary), then place the card in the first column on their paper. Next, they search for the capital and lowercase letter that matches the beginning sound in the name from within a whole basket of jumbled magnetic letters or letter tiles. Finally, they write the uppercase and lowercase letters in the last column.

***Differentiated practice*:** Encourage students who need more of a challenge to find all the letters in the name, mix and make the name three times, then write the name in the final column.

As weeks pass, more and more names accumulate in the box. Students know they must begin with the names we're studying this week, before moving on to practice with "review" names. Extend this activity, when your students are ready, to include searching for and writing *final* letters in the columns.

Read Max	Match Mm	Write Mm
Shelly	Sh	Sh
Becka	Bb	Bb

Figure 3.13 *Read, Match, & Write*

Easy-to-Make Name Cards

Class sets of cards, one for each student's name, are indispensible. You already have one set. If you attach your Name Wall names to your foam board with Velcro, they can be removed in a flash, used for activities, and easily re-posted. You'll find the following instructions helpful, as name cards are needed for several of the next activities:

- Type all your students' names into one Word document. "Select all," make the font bold, change the size, and print. Print several masters with fonts of varied sizes. Use the masters to run copies on cardstock, then laminate and cut.

- I make several small-, medium-, and large-font sets. Some of my activities call for small cards (made with 36-point font) like "Read, Match, & Write" on page 54. Meanwhile, a few very large sets (100-point font) are handy for activities in pocket charts.

- We have one set (made with 60-point font) on our magnetic whiteboard in the front of the class. Each laminated name card has a small magnet on the back. When students arrive in the morning, they find their name and place it in the proper place on our lunch count chart. We then use this set when we take class votes or complete Venn diagrams or graphs. This size works well for activities in centers, too.

- I use the sets all around the classroom. Instead of writing names on craft sticks and putting them in a can to manage taking turns, I dump a small class set of name cards in a can. I've accomplished the same goal, with less work!

Name Puzzles

Use one set of large-font name cards to make Name Puzzles. Cut each name into letters and store them in individual envelopes with the name written on the front. Place the name puzzles with the focus sounds of the week in a center. Students pick an envelope, read the name on the front (those who need help may look at the Name Wall to find a match and use the picture cue to read the name), then:

- dump the contents, mix the letters, and remake the name (using the Name Wall or the name written on the front of the envelope for aid, if needed);

- read the name;

- repeat: mix, make, and read three times;

- trace the name with a vis–à–vis marker;

- write the name, each letter just below the printed letter on the laminated card; and

- wipe the letters clean. Store them back in the envelope.

Our Name Puzzles get used over and over again, since I leave them in the center once each name has been studied. As is the rule with other activities, students know they must complete the Name Puzzles for the week first (those with the target letter-sound correspondences), before redoing Name Puzzles from previous weeks. If you find the need, include a copy of a student photo in each envelope for added support.

<table>
<tr><td>

Variation

After they've had several practice days with their Name Puzzles, have students mix, make, read, then write their name on paper, going through the steps as many times as possible in one minute. They love the challenge of trying to beat their score, so time them again. The rapid pace adds an element of fun!

</td></tr>
</table>

Here's a handy trick for the first week of school: Give each child his or her Name Puzzle and teach the procedure they'll use in the center. (This may be extended beyond the first week in kindergarten to help kindergartners learn to recognize the letters and read and spell their own names.) When it comes time to implement centers, you've already got one covered!

More Roll Call!

Place the featured name cards and photos of the week at the top of a pocket chart, creating a column for each different letter-sound correspondence. For example, *Felicia* creates the first column, *Max* and *Manuel* create the second column, and *Sam* and *Sebastian* make up the third. Place a set of large-font name cards in a box. Chant Roll Call (see page 40), randomly pick a name (reading the card to students, if needed), then substitute the initial sound with the first column's sound. So, *Dominica* becomes *Fominica*. Sort the name card under *Felicia*, using a capital F letter card to cover the *D*. Pick another name card, moving to the second column. Replace the initial sound with /m/, sort the card there, and cover the beginning with a capital M letter card. Move to the third column (in first grade) and repeat. Then start at the first column again, working through the class names, moving from one column to the next in turn. When finished, reread the chart of new names! (See Hint at left.) Use a stopwatch to time how long it takes, then read again, trying to increase your speed. Move the pocket chart to a center, so students can further manipulate the names, using the target sound-letter cards. Include a stopwatch in the center and they'll love reading and rereading those funny new names!

Hint

If needed, place students' photos next to their name cards to provide clues when rereading.

Word Hunts

I make a new Word Hunt poster featuring the target names and letter sounds each week. I fold a piece of poster paper into three columns. *Sam* and *Sebastian* are listed at the top of the first column, with the *s* underlined. *Manuel* and *Max* are at the top of the middle column, and *Felicia* is the header for the last column. We watch for words beginning with these letters in our reading and writing and share the pen (interactive writing) to record our first few examples, underlining the initial sound. Volunteers are then free to add to the poster. We review our findings a few times each week, inviting

Variation

Once you've thoroughly covered the beginning sounds in all students' names, complete Word Hunts searching for words matching the ending sounds in names.

Figure 3.14 *Windows for framing letters and words*

students to add to their own spelling dictionaries. Some teachers like to bind their Word Hunt posters together with binding rings, adding a page each week.

My students enjoy completing their own Word Hunts, too. Using a clipboard and window,* they read the room themselves or with a buddy and record words in the columns.

Letter Races

Hold up the name cards representing your target sounds of the week. Read each name with students, emphasizing the beginning sound. Remind students of the importance of knowing these letters and sounds by heart so they can use them to read and write new words. Letter races help us get to know letters and sounds by heart.

Each child needs a whiteboard and marker to race. If you don't have these, substitute plastic dinner plates with dry-erase markers or use scratch paper or individual chalkboards (something fun to race on makes the activity more exciting!). Direct them to write one of the week's uppercase and lowercase letters at the top of their boards as you model. Using the model (their racing letters should look as good as those top model letters), they race for 30 seconds, moving across their boards, writing the uppercase and lowercase letter as many times as possible (see Figure 3.15). When time is up, they tally their total and race one more time, again for 30 seconds, trying to beat their score. Before erasing the board, ask students, "Now who can tell us a word that starts with the sound that letter represents? Wow! That's a lot of words! No wonder we want to know this letter by heart! We'll use it a lot in our reading and writing!" Then, race on the next letter. Within just a few short minutes, you've reviewed the focus letters of the week!

Once students are skilled with beginning letters, race on ending letters.

> *** Free and Fast: Recyclable Windows!**
>
> *You know that kids are motivated to complete tasks when they have fun tools to use. Make windows for framing letters, words, or word parts during word hunts, or big book reading or while reading the room. Cut around the plastic address window of envelopes from your credit card, gas, electric, and water bills as shown in Figure 3.14. You can even laminate them if you wish. Since bills are a renewable resource, though, I'm not sure it's worth your time! Teach students how to make these windows (they can even decorate the wands to personalize them) and you'll always have a good supply!*

Figure 3.15 *Letter race on a whiteboard*

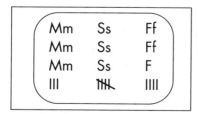

Figure 3.16 *Variation of a letter race*

> **Variation**
>
> *Have students make two or three columns on their board, writing the uppercase and lowercase letters of the week across the top. Using the model letters, they race across the columns writing, for example, Mm, Ss, Ff, Mm, Ss, Ff. They tally and race again to beat their score. Then, before cleaning the boards, have volunteers give words beginning with those sounds. The class repeats each word, then makes a tally or check mark in the column for the appropriate beginning letter. (See Figure 3.16.) Which letter sound was used to make the most words?*

Name-O

This is a variation of Pat Cunningham's popular Wordo (2008) with an important twist. Each student needs a 3-by-3 blank grid (alter this to whatever size is appropriate for your learners).

Ben	Bart	Shelly
Sam	Manuel	Becka
Max	Felicia	Sebastian

Figure 3.17 *Name-O grid*

Starting with the names of the week, students fill in the blanks with names from the Name Wall, creating their own unique bingo card. Then, the names from the Wall are removed, or a set of name cards is used to pick names at random. Rather than dispensing chips for students to mark their boards, we play the game in colored rounds. If we start with the red round, names that are called are traced in red until someone gets "Name-O!" We switch to a different color for each round. Now, students are more engaged, having to trace the name each time rather than just putting a chip down—easier management of children and materials and great practice, too!

Decodable Text

Though I'm not a huge fan of decodable texts, I understand their purpose, especially for children struggling to use phonetic cues in reading. The newer versions have more natural language, making them more appealing and more like real reading. Most reading programs include little books for guided reading and blackline masters for take-homes. Use the books that focus on the letter sounds you're emphasizing each week. Differentiate their use, ensuring strugglers have opportunities to read and reread them and take home the BLMs for more practice. Before they go home, have students highlight the words beginning with the target sounds.

For updated information on decodable text and current research, see Blevins (2006).

Guided Reading Word Work

When a group finishes a guided reading book, students find words beginning (later, ending) with the target letters of the week. These words are stretched and segmented using the concrete models illustrated in Chapter 1, each child using his or her own model. Then, students can write the beginning letter on the laminated elastic, Unifix, or zipper-pull models with vis-à-vis markers (write on, wipe off!). The clay models work well for this, too, since letters can be lightly carved into the pieces with toothpicks. Naturally, when students are ready to record more letters, encourage them to do so.

Figure 3.18 *Segmenting and blending words with a zipper-pull model*

Students found the name *Mike* and the words *mine, my,* and *mom* in their guided reading book and connected them to the names *Max* and *Manuel.* After segmenting and blending the words with their zipper-pull models, they moved the slide to the initial position and recorded the beginning letter *m* (see Figure 3.18).

Letter Search

Make single-page copies of familiar, favorite poems, rhymes, chants, and songs you've used for repeated shared readings. If the rhymes are long, shorten them (e.g., just copy the first stanza or the refrain or chorus on the page) so they are manageable for the reading level of your students. Slip them into page protectors. Students use vis-à-vis markers to circle the week's target letters as they reread, then wipe the page clean when they're through. Each time they find a letter, they record it on a graph (see "Letter Roll" on page 60).

Fun, inexpensive highlighting tool: Use transparent plastic index tabs (packaged in multiple bright colors in bags of 25 or so) to highlight letters, chunks, words, punctuation, and so on. (These are the tabs used by older students to create and index sections in school subject notebooks.) Use the tabs for center activities, but also for highlighting during shared and guided reading. They're great for the overhead, too!

Differentiate: More-able students can record the words they highlight rather than just the letter. Using a highlighting pen, they can then highlight the letter within the word on their record page.

Five little monkeys
jumping on the bed
one fell off and
bumped his head.

Figure 3.19 *Using highlighter tools for a letter search*

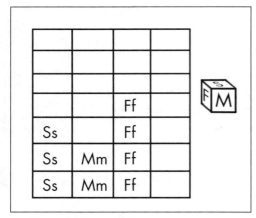

Figure 3.20 *Letter Roll*

Letter Roll

Make a game out of practicing letter formation. Program wooden cubes with the letters of the week. Students create a letter graph by rolling the die and recording the letter that comes up on large box graph paper. A letter wins when one fills a row or column. The same activity can be done if you program blank spinners with the key letters. Over time, you'll create a nice collection of letter dice and spinners. Students can use these for review once they've completed their graph for the week's focus.

Letter Sort

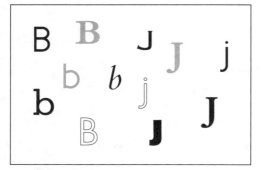

Figure 3.21 *Letter Sort*

Students learn letter features by sorting varied examples into rows below the name cards of the week. So, when working with Becka, Bahid, Bart, Justin, and Jenika, they sort uppercase and lowercase *b*'s and *j*'s. I use letters made from a variety of materials to keep interest high: bulletin board letters, fabric letters, magnetic letters, letter tiles, large letters in different fonts cut from magazines, buttons with letters written on them, tiny pasta letters, any kind of letters! Of course, letter sorts can be done with the final letters in names, too.

Anytime Alphabet Activities

These activities focus on *all* letters and sounds, not just those featured each week.

Like all kindergarten and first-grade teachers, I involve my class in a myriad of alphabet activities in addition to specific, targeted letter-sound lessons. We read and write alphabet books, sing alphabet songs; we eat, sleep, and breathe the alphabet in general! Here are some of my favorite alphabet activities involving names.

Concrete Models With Letters

Students love to get their hands on those concrete models from Chapter 1! Have them match generic examples to name cards. For example, using the elastic phoneme models, Sammi's name card is matched to one with four squares in different colors, whereas Juan's name is matched to one with three. Once the model is matched, students use it to segment and blend the name. Use the pipe cleaners with beads, Unifix cubes, and binding rings the same way. The models work for syllables, too. *Hernando* is matched with a three-block model, *Danielle* with two, and *Max* with one.

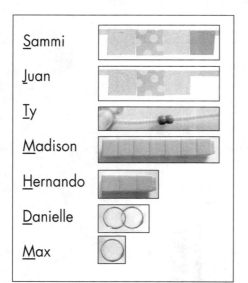

Figure 3.22 *Segmenting and blending with concrete models*

To add a phonics element to the match-up activity, students write letters on the models. They record letters for initial, final, and vowel sounds, or spell the complete names (in accordance with their abilities). They write on, wipe off (using vis-à-vis markers) on the laminated elastic, Unifix, or zipper-pull models or carve into clay as suggested for "Guided Reading Word Work." (See Figure 3.23.) Before erasing their work, they segment and blend the names.

Figure 3.23 *Adding phonics to the Match-Up activity*

Alternatively, you might permanently program an elastic model for the phonemes or syllables in each student's name, stapling a photo on the end. Students read the names and segment and blend the phonemes or syllables. (See Figure 3.24.)

Or, try this for more of a challenge: Fold back the photo cues and secure with paper clips. Students read each name, then self-check by looking at the photo. Make a few examples and have parent volunteers create the rest! (See Figures 3.25 and 3.26.)

Another example of a concrete model with letters:

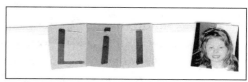

Figure 3.24 *Programmed model*

Figure 3.25 *An example at the syllable level*

Figure 3.26 *An example at the phoneme level*

Volunteers for Kid Smush can hold letter cards for the words you're segmenting and blending (just for the beginning, ending, or vowel sound or for the whole name). Now you're connecting the sound(s) to print!

Name Card Fold-Overs

Using one of your large-font (100-point) name card sets, hold up one name at a time, while folding the end of the word over the front, masking all but the beginning sound. (See Figure 3.27.)

Students predict the name and cross-check the letters as you slowly unmask the word parts. Be sure to turn the Name Wall around to the blank side, so students can't see the name cards and photos. They'll quickly develop great name-reading skills with this activity while they review letters and sounds. Additionally, you can call attention to simple chunks as they are unmasked. Work through four or five names in just two or three minutes!

Figure 3.27 *Name Card Fold-Over*

> **Variation**
>
> Make elastic models for words other than student names. Simply staple on a sticker or magazine photo for a picture cue or leave the cue off entirely. Elastic models are so fun to use, your students will read them again and again. You can use these models from year to year! Kids enjoy creating their own models for words, too.
>
>

Once students are proficient with one another's first names, you might work on last names. You can fold over the ends of other types of words on large flash cards, too. This is an easy way to work through masked word strategies without using any masking material. Though it's efficient, you don't have the benefit of a natural reading situation, as you do when masking words in connected reading materials (see "Masking" in Chapters 4 and 6).

Real-e Books

You'll find a remarkable, free, Internet-based book-making tool at www.realebooks.com. At the beginning of the year, I use Real-e Books to make a class photo and name book to reinforce alphabet and name recognition. I used to cut and paste to make the book . . . not any more! I'm not that tech-savvy; still, I've found Real-e Books very simple! Using the Real-e Book template, I just drop in a digital student photo, then type the text (which can be just the name or a repetitive sentence like *This is Bahid. This is Cathy.*). We read and reread this book like crazy and everyone gets a copy to take home. I keep extra copies in our "Favorite Rereads" book basket. Once you try Real-e Books, you'll be hooked. They're easy to make and can be used across the curriculum.

We create tons of other class books featuring digital photos and names for additional reinforcement. (We always underline the letter[s] for the beginning sound in each name.) For example, we've done one with Spanish words (e.g., *This is **K**enya's brazo*, with a photo of Kenya pointing to her arm); one after winter holiday, each child with a favorite gift (e.g., ***R**oberto loves his new helicopter*); and one for demonstrating numbers (e.g., ***A**drien shows two tens.* 10 + 10 = 20). These are absolute favorites for rereading and they're always checked out for family sharing!

Individual "Name Books" in Writing Workshop

Figure 3.28 *Name Book*

At the beginning of every year, students innovate on the simple class name Real-e Book I make to compose their own using the Name Wall. Some students sketch and label one classmate per page. Others try to write sentences. When these books are shared in the Author's Chair, everyone wants to do their own, which makes for great practice using the Name Wall!

Alphabet Strip Match-Up

Figure 3.29 *Alphabet Strip Match-Up with photos*

Students dump their set of class photos from their manila envelopes, mix them up, then try to quickly match the photos to the correct beginning letter on an alphabet strip. They say

> ### Variations
> - *Have students match ending sounds in names to the strip.*
> - *Have students match small name cards to the strip.*

the name, letter, and sound as they place the photo on the strip. This is another fun activity to time with students at their seats or in a center.

The same activities can be accomplished using a one-page alphabet grid rather than an alphabet strip. Students simply place the photo in the appropriate letter box.

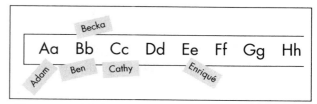

Figure 3.30 *Alphabet Strip Match-Up with name cards*

Big Book Name Match

As students reread familiar big books on their own or with a partner, they use a small-font name card set to try to match all the names with words that begin the same (later, end the same) in the book. When they find a match, they simply place the name card over the word and continue reading. They'll discover which names have the most common letter sounds and which have ones that are hard to match. When they're done reading, they lift the book and the names fall right out for cleanup! Which of your favorite big books have matches for all your names? It's fun to find out!

My Name, Your Name

Students match the letters in their name to letters in classmates' names. Each child's name is written boldly across the top of a piece of paper, with space between the letters to make columns. Then, they use a set of name cards in small font to

- find and sort only names that begin with the same letters as those in their name.

- find and sort only names that end with the same letters they have in their name.

- find and sort names with a letter from their name *in any position*.

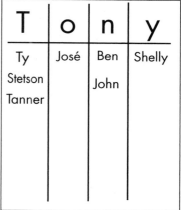

Figure 3.31 *My Name, Your Name*

Differentiate the task, based on what students need to practice. Also, make it easier by having them work with only a third or fourth of the class set at a time. Your more able students might write the names in the letter columns when they are done with the sort.

Letter Formation

Picking a name from a class set of large cards, students read the name, then trace over the beginning letter (letters for digraphs) with a finger. Then they form the letter, tracing over the name card multiple ways with Wikki Stix, pieces of yarn, beans, clay, and so on. Great tactile letter formation practice! Of course, students can later form the ending letter or whole names, too.

More Name Matching

There are all kinds of ways to mix and match names!

- Match student photos to name cards.
- Cut a class set of large name cards into syllables. Students match syllables to remake the names.
- Cut the beginning letter-sound correspondences off a set of name cards. Students match them back to remake the names.

If you have a large class, separate the name card sets into thirds or fourths and store the pieces in different envelopes. This way, students aren't dealing with pieces of all the names at once. Name matching is another activity students enjoy timing to improve their speed!

Sing the Wall/Cheer the Wall/Read the Wall

We love to sing the Name Wall by adapting different alphabet songs to sing names instead of letters. For instance, we sing one repetitive alphabet song like this, "A, B, C, Adam, Bahid, Catalina, D, E, F, Dominica, Evan, Felicia . . . ." We use the melody from the traditional alphabet song to sing our names. It's fun to tape record these renditions and play them in a listening center. Students can clap (wearing garden gloves for noise control), tap (using pencils or dowels with pom-poms on the ends), and point to letters on an alphabet strip or names on a list as they listen.

We also do a variety of Name Wall cheers to practice the names on the Wall during transition times. (You can find lists of cheers on the Internet. Just type "word wall cheers" into a search engine.) One of our favorites is the baseball cheer. We read a name and cheer the beginning letter (later the ending letter, then the whole spelling) while taking a swing with our imaginary baseball bats. Students will also read the Name Wall with fun pointers during read-the-room time.

Alphabet Book Tutoring

When I find students are falling behind grade-level benchmarks for mastering the alphabet, I assign each individual an upper-grade tutor. Tutors come to our classroom daily after lunch and work one-on-one to read a simple alphabet book with their tutee. Each page has the uppercase and lowercase letter and a picture of an object. The tutee reads the book (*Aa /a/ apple*), tracing each letter with his or her finger. The tutor provides help as needed. This quick, easy intervention works wonders to bring strugglers up to speed in a short amount of time.

Closing Thoughts

The name and alphabet activities in this chapter are designed to engage students while they build automaticity with letter names, forms, and letter-sound correspondences. Students rapidly learn letters and sounds through meaningful associations with classmates' names. You may be surprised at the ease with which this happens!

The next step is getting them to apply those letter sounds in their everyday reading and writing. That's where the "Significant Lessons for Guided Spelling and Decoding" come in. We'll go much farther than word play activities and typical Word Wall work. We'll actually make the Name Wall an indispensible tool for supporting students as they develop their spelling and decoding strategies.

CHAPTER 4

Significant Lessons for Guided Spelling and Decoding at the Emergent/Early Levels

What do we typically tell students when they are trying to spell a word? "Spell it how it sounds." "Is it on the Word Wall?" Simple pointers like these don't offer the scaffolding many learners need to successfully generate logical spellings for unknown words or to grow as spellers in general. The same can be said for decoding. Typically, when students are stuck on a word we offer, "Sound it out." This begs the question, "Well, *how do you sound it out?*"

Many teachers provide modeling, but fewer develop explicit, guided experiences that scaffold children through these processes. The following lessons are designed to meet that need. They aim to build students' facility with referring to the ABC Name Wall to help them spell and decode words while teaching and/or reviewing the strategies we use as good spellers and competent decoders.

Realize, these aren't just strategy lessons. Since we're referencing our names over and over, we're building letter-sound automaticity. When writing the letters is called for, we're working on letter formation, too.

The Lessons

Which Name?

Which Name? is designed to guide students through the steps of connecting to names (later, other words) on the Wall for spelling and decoding. It's a quick, oral transition activity. The

Important Points Pertaining to All the Lessons

These important points relate to adapting, managing, and getting the most out of each of the following lessons. When you're ready to try a lesson, you'll be more successful if you review the list.

- As with any other strategic process, you need to model the thinking involved in using the Name Wall during these lessons before turning responsibility over to students to respond. My first lessons are marked by language such as, "If I'm having trouble reading the word ___, I . . ." or "If I'm trying to spell ___, I . . ." I am as explicit as possible, detailing the process step-by-step. Use the dialogued examples to help you characterize your thinking, if needed.

- The lessons work well for whole group and small group. Naturally, you can tailor a lesson to meet more specifically the needs of a homogenous small group. The last lesson, "Sticky-Note Help," is designed to guide individuals.

- The lessons are meant to be repeated. Since they are short and quick (we work on only two or three words per lesson), they don't take a lot of time out of a day, but accumulate to a slew of experience over time. Students become very strategic when they have multiple opportunities to thoughtfully work through decoding and spelling new words across many reading and writing contexts.

- The difficulty level of each lesson is easy to change, since it is totally dependent on the complexity of the words you're spelling or decoding. Guide beginners to spell/decode three-letter words with short vowels (simple onsets, simple rimes like in *m-at*). Work on progressively longer words, with more complex onsets (*sp-at*, harder: *spl–at*), vowels (i.e., *ate*), and syllable patterns with experienced students. Another factor affecting difficulty is the familiarity of words. More-demanding vocabulary adds one more challenging element. More-advanced versions of each lesson are located in Chapter 6.

- When children experience difficulty identifying the sounds in the words you're guiding them to spell or blending the sounds in the words you're guiding them to read, they need more phonemic awareness practice. Refer to the ideas in Chapters 1 and 2 and regularly demonstrate and provide practice with the concrete models.

- Teach children to use wait- and think-time respectfully. When we're practicing our strategies to spell or decode new words, opportunities for learning are lost if students quickly call out answers. I explain to students, "Remember, when we're working together to figure out a word, everyone must wait until we reveal all the clues. We want everyone to have a chance to use and develop their strategies. If someone blurts out the word (or spelling), our chance to talk about what we do as readers (or spellers) is gone. We need to support one another's learning by being respectful of think-time."

- One way I manage this is to use the "five-finger rule." Once we've worked through a word, I tell the class to "wait for five fingers," which gives everyone some final think-time before a word is read or spelled. I slowly hold up the fingers on one hand, one at a time. When all five are up, everyone can call out the answer.

- Be explicit when introducing a lesson and debrief afterward. Begin each lesson with an explanation for why you're practicing what you're practicing. End the lesson with a quick review and/or questions such as, "Okay, readers, when would you use these steps to figure out a word?" or "How does this help you as a reader?" "Spellers, what did we do to come up with a logical attempt for this word?" or "How does this help you as a speller?" These are purposeful lessons. We want our students to adopt these strategies for their independent reading and writing until they're proficient enough to no longer need the Word Wall. So really drive these points home.

- We're using names as first Word Wall words then adding other words to cover more letter-sound correspondences. All the lessons and activities work exactly the same way whether analogies are being made to names or other words. No adjustments are required.

- Lastly, there is one big, burning question everyone who has a Word Wall asks, "What do you do if you're in the middle of a lesson and you don't have a word you need on your Wall?" My answer: if you don't have a word to connect to, simply supply one for students or ask them if they have one in their heads. For example, if we're spelling the word *jewel* and we don't have a j name on our Name Wall, I might say, "I know a name that starts like that: *Jill (I write it on the board)*. If this is *Jill*, how should we start the word *jewel?*"

example below is on an emergent level. It shows what I might do early on in kindergarten or with beginning English language learners when the goal is to get students hearing and representing sounds at the beginnings of words (developmentally spelling *s* for *seal* and *r* for *rooster*, for example). See "Adapting the Lesson" for more advanced learners.

Spelling Example

As students are gathering on the carpet, I move the ABC Name Wall front and center and say,

> We use the names on our Name Wall frequently to help us spell words we don't know. Let's practice for just a minute so you can use the Wall quickly and easily. Let's say we're writing a letter in Writing Workshop to tell the principal thanks for the pizza party our class won in last week's contest. I want to tell him the pizza was yummy. Which name on the Wall will help me write the letter for the first sound in the word *yummy*? Remember to do what good spellers do: say the word slowly, stretching out the first sound and putting the brakes on when you say it. Then think, which name do I know that sounds the same?

Students orally stretch /yyyyy/ ummy and scan the Wall for the analogous name. After wait-time, I ask for responses.

Students: Yolanda! *[pointing to the name on the wall]*

Ms. Wag: Yep! /Yyyyy/ olanda starts with the same sound and the same letter as *yummy*. What letter do we need then?

Students: Y! *[If students cannot identify the letter, name it and point it out on the name card. Model generating the spelling by writing* y *on the board while discussing proper letter formation.]*

Ms. Wag: Great! Now, if we want to spell *pizza*, which name will help us? *[Wait-time.]*

Students: Patrick! *[pointing to the name on the wall]*

Ms. Wag: Yes, /Ppppp/ atrick starts with the same sound and the same letter as *pizza*. What is that letter?

Students: P! *[I model spacing between the words, writing* p. *Then model rereading while pointing to the letters* y *and* p, *"Yummy pizza."]*

Ms. Wag: It's important to be able to hear the connections between sounds in words we're trying to write and sounds in names we know; that's why we practice "Which Name?" See how the Name Wall helps us write new words?

Figure 4.1 *Using the Name Wall to find beginning letters of words we want to spell*

Continue to guide students to use connections to generate other spellings.

Adapting the Lesson

When students can hear and represent more than initial sounds in their writing, or it's time to push their development in that direction, address hearing connections to other prominent sounds in the word you're trying to write. For example, after writing the *y* for *yummy*, I might say, "We have *y* for the beginning sound in *yummy*. As you stretch the word further *[demonstrating with a concrete model]*, can you hear any other sounds inside it? *[Students say /mmmm/.]* Yes, I hear and feel /mmmmm/, too. Is there a name on our Wall that can help us with /mmmmm/?"

If you have a name to connect to, move forward, recording the letter on the board. Students may surprise you, offering connections to sounds inside names other than in the initial position ("*Tammy* has /mmmmm/!"). If this happens, great! Use what they find. If you don't have an analogous name, provide one. ("We don't have a name on our Wall with /mmmmm/, but I have a friend, Mike, and he spells his name this way: [*writing on the Magna Doodle*] *M-i-k-e*.")

Once the letter *m* is identified, I write it next to *y*. Then, I may ask for more connections. Students may likely say they hear /eeeee/ at the end of yummy and offer the letter *e* as a spelling. *Y-m-e* makes a good letter-name spelling (Bear, Invernizzi, Templeton, & Johnson, 2007) for *yummy*, and as long as I know I'm pushing their development forward, we're on the right track.

How do I know I'm pushing spelling development forward? Examine students' writing. If most are recording letters for initial sounds, it's time to start making connections to ending sounds. If they're representing ending sounds, push for prominent medial sounds. Their writing will show what they can do and what they can't. Be sure to use the concrete models to lend support along the way. Students need to see how to listen inside words beyond their current level of understanding. Additionally, when you observe students falling behind their peers as evidenced in their writing, it's time to plan some small-group intervention at their level.

yme pza

Figure 4.2 *Hearing and writing more sounds and letters in words*

> ### Variation
>
> *Students can also write the letters during Which Name? All they need is a whiteboard or scratch paper. They can show their response to the teacher or a buddy, saying which name helped them with the letter(s) and the steps taken to get there can be reviewed just as in the dialogue on page 68.*

> ### Note
>
> *The purpose of this lesson is quick, strategic practice to bolster students' independent spelling abilities. If our goal was to publish writing, displaying it in the classroom for rereading, for example, the spellings would be recorded correctly on the final product. See "Interactive Writing" in Chapter 6 for more on this issue.*

Decoding Example

Which Name? is also a strategic decoding lesson. This example is for emergent readers.

Ms. Wag: Boys and girls, as we read, we all come across words we don't know. Let's practice what good readers do when this happens. Pretend we are reading along and we come to this unknown word. [*I write the word* sat *on a Magna Doodle*.] Which name on our Name Wall would help us begin to read this word? Do you see any names that look the same at the beginning? Think-time . . .

Students: Santos!

Ms. Wag: Yes, Santos begins with the same letter. So, if we know /Sssss/ antos' name, what sound does this word begin with? [*I point to* sat.]

Students: /Sssss/!

Ms. Wag: That's right! If this is /Sssss/antos [*I point to the name card*], then this is [*running a finger under the letter s*] /sssss/. What about the last letter in the word? Which name can help us? Think-time . . .

Students: Tanner!

Ms. Wag: Right! If this is /Tttttt/ anner [*I point to the name card*], then this is [*running a finger under the letter t in* sat] /ttttt/. So, the sounds we know in this word are /sssss/ . . .? [*I run a finger under the letters.*]

Students: /Ttttt/!

Ms. Wag: Great! And, here we have /aaaaa/. [*I point to* a.] We blend those sounds together /sssss/ /aaaaa/ /ttttt/ [*demonstrating with a concrete model*] to read the word *sat*.

After guiding students to decode one or two more simple, three-letter words, debrief "How did the Name Wall help us read these words?" (Also see Variations, below.)

Adapting the Lesson

Naturally, with more advanced learners, connections should be made to the vowel, as well: "This word has two letters at the beginning just like /Sssss aaaaa ntos/. If this is /Sssss aaaaa ntos/, then this is [*pointing to* sat] /sssss aaaaa/. Which name will help us with that ending sound?" Additionally, at this stage, I begin to show children how chunks work in words. We'd look at how P̲a̲t̲rick could help us read *sat* (see Chapters 5 and 6).

Note

Once you're extending your ABC Wall to include non-name words, ask students "Which word will help me?" since they can connect to a name or other type of word from the Wall.

Name Wall Race

Name Wall Races are inspired by the fact that if students can't *find* words on the Wall, they can't use them to make connections for spelling or decoding. When I began using Word Walls in my classroom, I assumed kids could automatically locate the words they needed. Once I realized they need support to develop referencing skills (after all, over time many words are on the Wall!), Word Wall Races became part of our routine. Kids love to race to find words and working through the process in a guided fashion helps them use the Wall more efficiently!

Here's how it works: Two volunteers come forward to flank the Word Wall, one on each side. They are given prompts and think-time for the name they will race to find. To keep everyone active, the class also races to find the name, writing it (or the first or last letter, depending on their abilities) on scratch paper or a whiteboard. On "Go!" the two racers shine their laser pointers to race for the name. The winner stays standing for another round while the other student passes the pointer to a classmate who recorded the correct word/letter.

Variations

Show simple titles on the covers of emergent books, shielding the picture with a piece of cardstock. Work to decode the main word of the title (e.g., with Hairy Cat, *we work together to read the word* cat). *Once you've guided children to make connections to letter sounds and names on the Wall to read the main word on the cover, reveal the picture and confirm the word. Again, if you find you don't have an analogous name on your Wall, simply provide one. After working through a few words, debrief: "How did we figure out those unknown words?" Be sure to note how the picture clues were helpful once revealed.*

While a new volunteer is coming forward for the next race, we quickly debrief. "How did you find the name you needed?" "What made you look there?" This way, we review good spelling and decoding strategies while also going over techniques for quickly locating words.

Spelling Example

Ms. Wag: Boys and girls, let's say I'm writing in my learning log about one of the chickens we hatched. There's a name on the ABC Wall that will help me write the first letters in *chicken*. Think. [*wait-time*] One, two, three . . . GO! Class, which of our racers found the correct name first?

Students: Jose!

Ms. Wag: Jose, how did you find the name you needed?

Jose: I said *chicken* out loud and put the brakes on after the /ch ch ch/. Then, I thought, *Charlie* sounds the same.

Ms. Wag: Great, so you said the word, drawing out that first sound and connected it with *Charlie*! Class, what letters would you need then for the first sound in *chicken*?

Students: C-h! [*Remember,* ch *is underlined on* Charlie's *name card to aid recognition that the two letters stick together to make one sound.*]

Ms. Wag: Yes, if this is /Chchchchch arlie/ with the letters *c-h*, then /chchchchch icken/ is spelled with *c-h*, too. Think about where you find Charlie's name on the Wall: at the beginning, middle, or end of the alphabet? If you don't recognize the name card, use Charlie's photo to help you find it.

As a new volunteer is picked (one who has *c-h* or the name *Charlie* on his or her whiteboard), you can extend the lesson as I do below.

Ms. Wag: Did anyone make any other connections to names on the Wall that would help us write *chicken*?

Student: I hear /kkkkk/ like *Kenya*.

Ms. Wag: Yes! /Kkkkk/ is a sound I hear in the middle of *chicken* and, sure enough, you need the letter k just like *Kenya*!

Student: /Nnnnn/ like *Nathan*!

Ms. Wag: Yes! Nathan's name has /n/ at the beginning and the end! If this is /Nnnnn atha nnnnn/ with the letter *n*, then I must need the letter n for the last letter in *chickennnnn*.

As sounds, names, and letters are connected, you might write the letters on the board to show the emerging spelling: chkn.

Decoding Example

Ms. Wag: We're going to race to find names that will help us read new words. Remember, when I show you the unknown word, if you can read it already, don't say it! Everyone needs a chance to work on their strategies for figuring out new words, and if someone reads the word aloud, the chance is gone. Okay, say I'm reading along and I come to this word I don't know [*I show the word on the chalkboard, overhead, or Magna Doodle:* dog]. Which name on the Wall will help me begin to sound out this word? Think. [*wait-time*] One, two, three . . . GO!

Students: Sammi got it!

Ms. Wag: Yes, I see Sammi pointing to the name *Dominica*. Sammi, why did you pick *Dominica*?

Sammi: I saw the d just like *Dominica* in the word on the board.

Ms. Wag: What does that tell you about this word?

Sammi:	It starts like /Ddddd ominica/ with /ddddd/.
Ms. Wag:	Yep! [*As a new volunteer is coming forward to race,*] Does anyone see any other connections to names on the Wall?
Student:	I see *g* like in *Grace.*
Ms. Wag:	Exactly, so this word has [*pointing to the letters in the word on the chalkboard*] /ddddd/ — /ggggg/. Let's read the word together:
All:	[*While I point*] /dddd/
Ms. Wag:	[*Voicing the vowel sound,*] /ooooo/
All:	/ggggg/. Dog!
Ms. Wag:	Great job, readers! We know once we figure out the individual sounds, we have to blend them together to read the word. [*I demonstrate blending /d/, /o/, /g/ with a concrete model.*] For this word we saw the first letter matched /Ddddd ominica/ and the last letter matched /Ggggg race/. If you were reading in a book, you would have the sentence to help you and maybe a picture clue, too. Sounding out /ddddd/ /ggggg/ [*I point to the letters in the word on the board*] and seeing a picture of a dog will help any good reader read the word *dog*!

Note

Remember, the lessons in this chapter are examples on emergent and early levels. It is vitally important to teach children to use **all** the letter sounds in words as their skills develop, so they become efficient decoders and spellers.

When you're finished racing on a few words, don't forget the importance of debriefing. "Why do we take the time to do Word Wall Races? We all come across words we don't know how to read (or spell). The Word Wall Race lets us talk about and practice what good readers (or spellers) do to read new words . . ."

Keep in mind, the difficulty of these lessons is easily changed by the complexity of the words being spelled and/or read. Consider using the same lessons in small groups to more accurately pinpoint students' needs.

Variation

Using the titles of simple emergent books, as recommended with Which Name?, incorporates picture cues to help your readers and places strategic practice in a real reading context.

Decoding Lesson: Masking

We all come to words we don't know when we're reading. To help us with this, each week, I'm going to cover a few words in big books, in the morning message, or on our shared reading posters, so we can work together to practice what good readers do when they come to a word they don't know in something they're reading.

This simple introduction sets the scene for lots of effective decoding practice across all kinds of shared-reading contexts. Students get so excited when they see a masked word. They're eager to figure it out like they're slowly opening a tiny present!

I make sure to mask words in "fresh" reads so students can't rely on memory. Let's look at an example from the big book *Miss Bindergarten Gets Ready for Kindergarten.* We're in the process of reading together when we come to a page with a covered word:

All:	"Gwen McGunny packs her . . ."
Ms. Wag:	Oh! It's a covered word! What would fit and make sense here?
Student:	Rabbit!
Ms. Wag:	Yes, *rabbit* does fit and make sense. I also see a rabbit in the picture. Good readers use what fits and makes sense and picture clues to help them read new words. So, if the covered word is *rabbit*, what letter would you expect to see, boys and girls?
Students:	*R* like *Roberto*.
Ms. Wag:	That's right. If this word is /rrrrr abbit/, it will start with the letter *r* just like /Rrrrr oberto/! [*I pull back the first part of the masking tape, to reveal the first letter, b.*] Oh, it's not the letter *r*. Do we have a name on our Wall that starts like this?
Students:	Becka!
Ms. Wag:	Yes, *Becka* starts with the letter *b*. So, the first sound in this word is . . .?
Students:	/Bbbbb/!
Ms. Wag:	Let's reread, then, using this beginning sound and thinking about what fits and makes sense and the picture. "Gwen McGunny packs her /bbbbb/ . . ."
Students:	Bunny!
Ms. Wag:	Okay, *bunny* fits and makes sense. If the covered word is *bunny*, what other letters would you expect to see?
Students:	*N* like *Nathan*!
Ms. Wag:	Yep, I also hear /nnnnn/ in bunnnnnny. [*I slowly, unmask to show* b-u-n *as students cheer.*] Now, what letter might we see for that ending sound?
Student:	*E* like *Charlie*.
Student:	*Y* like *Shelly*.
Mrs. Wag:	Could be, let's see. [*I unmask the* y.] The word *bunny* ends with the letter *y* like *Shelly*. Wow! You did a super job using reading strategies to figure out that unknown word. First, we thought of what would make sense using the picture, since we couldn't see any letters. Then, when I uncovered the *b*, you connected to /Bbbbb ecka/ so you knew the beginning sound in the word was /bbbbb/. Then, everyone said *bunny* and we carefully studied the other letter sounds in the word to make sure we were right! You know what else would help us in this book? The rhyming! On each page, something rhymes with the character's name. That's a big clue because *bunny* rhymes with *Gunny*!

Once we've summed up our method, we read on in our book. The process is quick and, when done repeatedly, really pays off. Now students really see what we mean when we say, "Sound it out!" This makes all the difference in the world!

Lesson Notes

Post-it tape or the sticky part of sticky notes are perfect for masking words since they're easily removed without leaving residue on books or posters. You can mask words on overhead transparencies, too. Try a page from your science, math, or social studies book. Students need to understand that these strategies work in anything they're reading.

Variations

Try masking different parts of
words, rather than whole
words every time. For
example, show the initial letter,
final letter, or prominent
chunk, but mask the rest of
the word.

There's a real magic to the question, "If it's _____ (students' prediction for the covered word), *what letter(s) do you expect to see?*" When you ask this before unmasking a word part, you force children to think through the word, segment it into sounds using phonemic awareness, and connect those sounds to letters on the Name Wall.

Adapting the Lesson

With less experienced readers, figuring out the beginning sound in the word while using the other cues may be enough work, while I'd note the *un* chunk in *bunny* with more experienced readers (see Chapters 5 and 6 for chunking).

Spelling Lesson: High-Speed Spelling

This is another purposeful student favorite. I often do High-Speed Spelling when calling the class to the rug. Holding up the Magna Doodle, I ask for a volunteer: "We're stuck! Can you help us write the word *lunch*?"

The class slowly and quietly counts to five, giving the volunteer five seconds. (This is "high speed" spelling, after all, which adds an element of fun; but, you can certainly increase to ten seconds, if you choose.) The student writes the letters he or she can and tells us which names on the Wall are helpful. For example, if Ernesto writes *l-ch* on the Magna Doodle, he may report, "*L* like *Lucio* and *c-h* like *Charlie*."

Great! Ernesto heard the beginning sound /lllll/ in /lllll unch/ and connected to /Lllll ucio/. He also heard the ending sound /chchchchch/ and connected it to /Chchchchch arlie/. That's just what a good speller would do—stretch the word out to hear the sounds inside it and think of other words he knows to help him write the letters for those sounds. Did anyone else make a connection to the sounds in /lllll uuuuu nnnnn chchchchch/? [*I segment the word with a concrete model.*]

Discuss any other connections to names on the Wall. Also, depending on your students' abilities, you might write the correct spelling of *lunch* at the bottom of the Magna Doodle before calling up another volunteer to spell a different word.

Note

Why say, "We're stuck"? We
use the strategy of segmenting
words into sounds and
connecting to other words
only to spell unknown words.
If you already know how to
spell a word, you just write it
automatically.

If you find students are struggling, guide them with an elastic model to segment the word before beginning the five- (or ten-) second count. Remember, difficulty here means more work on phonemic awareness is needed.

When students represent only the beginning sound in the word, you can certainly push development by thinking aloud (using a concrete model) to hear and connect to the ending sound or other sounds in the word, adding to the Magna Doodle yourself. But be sure to praise what the student was able to do first.

One of the great things about High-Speed Spelling is we can work through a few words, reviewing critical strategies, in just a few minutes!

Challenge Words

I like to do Challenge Words at least once a week as the mini-lesson to open Writing Workshop. This sets the stage for the independent writing students are about to undertake.

As we write, we often want to use words we don't know how to spell. That's why we do Challenge Words. We have to know what to do as writers to get those words down on paper. We have to know how to give them a good, logical try, even if they aren't spelled correctly. Challenge Words lets us practice our spelling strategies together so we can feel confident using them. For example, Rezonne's been working on a zoo alphabet book. He was stuck on the word *tiger*. If you were writing the challenging word *tiger*, what would you do? Give it a try on your paper.

[*After wait-time,*] Okay, great spellers, what did you come up with for *tiger*? A lot of kids your age wouldn't even try to write *tiger* because it's a pretty tough word. [*Students call out their spellings for* tiger, *and I record a few of their attempts on the board.*]

I heard these different spellings for *tiger*. I'll run my finger under each and we'll test to see if it is a good try. Remember, when you spell a new word, you should do the same thing. Run your finger under it and sound through what you wrote to check how you did. You may decide a letter is missing or there's something else you want to change.

t r

I see this speller heard the beginning sound in *tiger* and wrote the letter *t* just like in Tineka's name. He also heard /rrrrr/ at the end of /tige rrrrr/, just like in Roberto's name. So, *t-r* is a great try for tiger since it correctly represents the beginning and ending sounds in the word. [*Note: I like to pull the names off the Wall as I reference them, holding them up right next to the attempt so it's easy to see the connections. Additionally, as always, it helps to have a concrete model to visually demonstrate where the sounds are heard within the word.*]

ch r

This speller has the /rrrrr/ at the end, but started with /ch/ like Charlie. /Ch/ can be confused with /t/. One way to know the difference is to feel it. Everyone say /ttttt iger/ with me. Now say /Ttttt ineka/. Notice how your lips are apart and your tongue is tapping the roof of your mouth just behind your top teeth as you voice /ttttt/. Now say /Chchchchch arlie/ /chchchchch/. Notice how your lips are pushed out? /Ch/ feels different, doesn't it? We need the letters *c-h* /ch/ for words like *chip, chocolate, change,* and *chicken*, but we need the letter *t* for /ttttt iger/. Good job on that last letter. We need *r* for /rrrrr/ at the end of *tiger*.

t g r

I see this speller heard the beginning /ttttt/, the ending /rrrrr/, and a middle sound /ggggg/ just like *Grace*. He's pushing himself to hear and try letters for *more* sounds in the word he is trying to spell.

t y g r

The beginning of this spelling reminds me of Mylee's name. If Mylee's name has /my/ and is spelled *m-y*, *t-y* seems like a good attempt for /ti/ /ger/. I see this speller also heard the /ggggg/ and /rrrrr/. [*I point to* g *and* r.]

Talk through simpler attempts before moving to more-complex samples. When you get a variety of attempts, as in this example, the lesson is multilevel. Different students will take away different learning, depending on where they are developmentally as spellers. After working through a few student attempts on one word, have the class undertake one more-challenging word (I typically have kindergartners try two words, while we do three later in the year in first and second grades). Students benefit so much from analyzing one another's examples. Peer modeling is a highly influential learning tool.

Once your students move beyond letter-name spelling, end your examination of each word by showing the correct spelling. Talk it through syllable by syllable. This is demonstrated in the more advanced Challenge Word lesson in Chapter 6.

As you close the lesson, be sure to debrief: "How does practicing Challenge Words help us in our own writing? What steps do we use to attempt a challenging word?"

Sticky-Note Help

Here's a strategic way to provide significant help to *individuals* stuck on spelling or decoding a word without doing all the work for them.

Spelling Example

K student: Ms. Wag, how do you spell *beach*?

Ms. Wag: Are there any names on the Wall that sound like *beach* at the beginning?

Student: I don't know.

Ms. Wag: Say *beach* slowly, putting the brakes on after that first sound. [*I provide assistance with a concrete model, if necessary. Again, students having trouble identifying sounds in words in accordance with developmental standards need more work with phonemic awareness activities like those in Chapters 1 and 2.*]

Student: /B/ /b/.

Ms. Wag: That's it! Who's name starts with /bbbbb/?

If the student provides a name, write it on a sticky note, underlining the *b*. If the student cannot provide an analogous name, write one on the sticky note, underlining the *b*.

Ms. Wag: So, if this is /Bbbbb art/ [*pointing to the word on the sticky note*], what letter do you need to begin the word /bbbbb each/?

Student: *B*!

Ms. Wag: Right on! Here's the sticky note to help you.

If appropriate, direct the student to identify the ending sound in the word, adding an analogous name to the sticky note with the *ch* underlined.

Decoding Example

First-grade student: What's this word [*pointing to* sister *in a book*]?

Ms. Wag: What is that first sound?

Student: I don't know.

Ms. Wag: Does it look the same at the beginning as anyone's name on our Name Wall?

Student: I don't know.

Ms. Wag: Whose name is this [*writes* Santos *on a sticky note*]?

Student: Santos. [*If the student can't read the name, run your finger under it, read it and have her repeat.*]

Ms. Wag: If this is /Sssss antos/, then the first sound in this word is . . .?

Student: /Sssss/!

Ms. Wag: Yep, /sssss/, and here's another /sssss [*pointing to the second s in* sister]. Then, whose name looks like this [*pointing to the* t]?

Student: Tyler!

Ms. Wag: Yes [*writes Tyler on the note*]. So, if this is Tyler, then this is [*pointing to the* t *in* sister]?

Student: /Ttttt/.

Ms. Wag: Sound through what we have so far then.

Together: /Sssss/ /sssss/ /ttttt/.

Student: /Rrrrr/!

Ms. Wag: Yep, /rrrrr/ just like /Rrrrr oberto/! We also see the letter *r* at the end of *Tyler*. Let's try all the sounds together.

Together: Sssss/ /sssss/ /ttttt/ /rrrrr/.

Student: *Sister*!

Ms. Wag: Let's go back and read the sentence to make sure *sister* makes sense.

Together: *This is my sister.*

Ms. Wag: See how the names on the Wall helped you sound out that word?

For two more advanced examples, see Sticky-Note Help in Chapter 6.

Don't miss my demonstration lessons incorporating both the ABC Name Wall and the Chunking Wall with emergent/early learners (Masking on page 109 and Interactive Writing on page 116). They are placed there since they must follow our discussion of chunks in Chapters 5 and 6.

Closing Thoughts

Using students' names to connect letters and sounds isn't complicated. The lessons in this chapter aim to support students in using classmates' names (later, other words) to read and write new words at the emergent and early levels. The payoffs for early success are enormous: " . . . it is difficult to overstate the importance of getting children off to an early successful start in reading. We must ensure that students' decoding and word recognition abilities are progressing solidly. Those who read well are likely to read more, thus setting an upward spiral into motion" (Cunningham & Stanovich, 2001, p. 148). I've offered my best lessons here for providing intelligent, guided practice for spelling and decoding development within real literacy contexts. Repeated experience with the significant lessons is truly powerful. This explicit approach gives students the support they need to experience reading and writing success and set that "upward spiral into motion"!

CHAPTER 5

The Chunking Name Wall for Literacy Learners at the Early/Developing Levels

It's Lucio's second week in second grade. He stops reading his book to come up to me for help on an unknown word.

"What's this word?" he asks, pointing to *wetter*. "/Wwwww/ ?" he looks up at me.

"What's the first chunk you see in the word? Remember, the chunk is the vowel and what comes after." (I point to the first chunk, covering the rest of the word with my finger.)

"E-t?" (He spells the chunk.)

"Yep! Is there a name on our Wall with that chunk? Look under the e chunks."

"Stetson!"

"Yes! Since we know /Stet/ (pause) /son/, the *e-t* chunk says . . . ?"

"/Et/!"

"You've got it! So, the first part of the word you're reading is (still covering the second syllable with my finger) . . . ?"

"Wet!"

"Great! What's the next chunk in the word?" (I point to it for extra support.)

"E-r."

"Whose name . . . " (Lucio interrupts me before I finish my question.)

"Perla!"

"Right! Perla has /er/. So, the word you are reading is /wet/ . . . ?"

"/Er!/ Wetter!"

"Exactly! You did a super job using the chunks from the names on our Wall to read the chunks in this new word. Now, read the sentence again to make sure *wetter* makes sense."

Teaching with the Name Chunking Wall is just that simple and rewarding. Like Lucio, your students will catch on to connecting to the chunks in classmates' names quickly and easily. If the simplicity of this strategy appeals to you, think how it will appeal to your students!

When I wrote my first book about teaching children to use chunks to decode and spell, the concept was not well known. I was going out on a professional limb, trying something new no one in my school or district was implementing. I was fed up with traditional phonics methods, which 20 years ago consisted of teaching tons of rules for sounding out words and decoding letter-by-letter. These approaches left several of my second graders bewildered. I stuck closely to a prescribed curriculum consisting of phonics worksheets and scripted lessons, but when I found my students' reading and writing abilities weren't improving, I knew something had to change.

Luckily, I was reading Marilyn Jager Adams's hot-off-the-press *Beginning to Read: Thinking and Learning About Print* (1990) for a master's class. Therein, she wrote about word recognition research involving chunks, summarizing findings that made a lot of sense to me, especially given my students' frustrations. Of particular interest was how chunks are consistent and reliable; the vowel sounds almost always remain the same from word to word. Additionally, blending and segmenting these larger word parts to decode and spell was shown to be much easier than working with tiny, sometimes elusive phonemes.

Immediately, I planned changes to our literacy curriculum to include demonstrations showing how to use chunks in real reading and writing. The children made amazing progress that I gleefully documented in literacy profiles. My excitement for these strategies has only grown over the years as I've developed more and more common-sense ways to incorporate chunking into meaningful instruction. And, sure enough, strategically teaching analogy is now widespread, with phonograms, rimes, spelling patterns (all terms commonly used for chunks) appearing in almost every major reading program on the market today. Research shows, "Knowledge of within-word patterns affords greater efficiency and speed in reading, writing, and spelling" (Bear et al., 2007). Using students' names to introduce and reinforce the magic of chunking makes the process even more successful and meaningful. Motivation soars when kids see how chunks from their own names help them read and write new words so easily!

Note

For more detail on this fascinating research and how it relates to traditional phonics practice, or to check out my early students' amazing progress, see my book Phonics That Work: New Strategies for the Reading/Writing Classroom *(Scholastic, 1994). Additionally, Marilyn Adams's book cited above is still a very timely read.*

Another Note

Be sure to review the key terms in the appendix if you are new to the idea of chunking and analogy.

Grade-Level Relevance

The idea of chunking resonates with children. It's easy to understand and apply. Using chunks to sound out words diminishes the problems of the variability of the sounds of individual letters (especially vowels) and the arduousness of blending and segmenting those minute phonemes from letter-by-letter decoding and spelling (Adams, 1990; Wagstaff, 1994, 1999). Logic tells us to start showing students how chunks work once they

- have a basic understanding of the alphabet.
- have facility with rhyming (so they can hear and understand the connection among chunks).
- have phonemic awareness of beginning and ending sounds in short words.
- utilize initial and final letter-sound correspondences in short words when reading and writing.
- are beginning to represent and use vowels in their reading and writing.

However, this is not to say students must have a *mastery* of the above before working with rimes. Just as phonemic awareness continues to develop as students work with the alphabet, the skills on our list can and will develop right alongside a curriculum that includes chunking, as long as critical teaching points are made and guided practice is regularly available at students' levels. If students are still struggling with rhyming, for instance, working with rimes on the Chunking Name Wall will boost their abilities. Likewise, if they're experiencing difficulty segmenting words into onset, rime, and phonemes or hearing vowel sounds, the instructional activities involving chunks will help.

With beginning English language learners and in kindergarten and first grade, it makes sense to begin the year with an ABC Name Wall, since our main focus is teaching or reviewing the alphabet. In my classroom experience, I've been comfortable mentioning chunks in modeling and shared reading and writing around the middle point of the kindergarten year and directly teaching analogy with a simple kindergarten Chunking Wall by the fourth term. Indeed, most commercial reading programs begin introducing short-vowel phonograms in late kindergarten. Chunking comes up much sooner in first grade. Once we've thoroughly reviewed the alphabet, we're ready to add rimes into the mix. This happens in many first-grade classes around the beginning of the second term (assuming a four-term school year).

How are Word Walls handled, then, when you are ready to start chunking with beginning English language learners and in kindergarten and first grade? My best advice is to begin a separate Word Wall on a new piece of foam board rather than doing away with or changing the ABC Name Wall. Many students, particularly those who struggle, will need more time to reference the names at the alphabet level and it's easy to continue modeling, instruction, and practice when that Wall is still available. Some teachers like the idea of using highlighting tape to call attention to the useful chunks in students' names on the ABC Name Wall, rather than having two Word Walls. But this may confuse some students and doesn't make for the easiest referencing. I keep the ABC and Chunking Walls separate and teach children to look to the appropriate foam board based on their needs. If they need to find a chunk, they look to the Chunking Name Wall where the names are organized according to the first vowel in the rime (see page 84). This makes it easier for children to locate and use words they need (as I'll explain).

I think the separation of the foam boards lends clarity to instruction and practice, as well. When working with emergent guided reading groups, I'll pull over the ABC Name Wall, knowing we're practicing connecting to the beginning and ending sounds in words as we work with our little books. I may use this foam board to section off a space in the room for an alphabet center for this group, as well. While working with advanced groups, I'll pull up the Chunking Name Wall instead, since these students already have automaticity with the alphabet and its use. As follow-up, they may be assigned to work with the Chunking Name Wall in a center. You won't regret the extra time or space needed to have two Word Walls, since not much of either is required and I'm sure you'll see the wisdom of this method as you and your class work with the Walls.

As a second-grade teacher and with more developed English language learners, I begin the year with a Chunking Name Wall, knowing not all my students are completely solid with the alphabet. Again, I'm comfortable with this because I know their phonemic awareness and phonics skills will continue to grow as they are immersed in instruction in how words work and given plenty of appropriate leveled practice. Additionally, just because the names are organized by chunk doesn't mean we can't reference connections at the alphabet level, too. I recall having several second graders who struggled with /sh/ one school year. Having Shaday as a classmate was really convenient as we referenced the onset in her name a lot!

Getting Started

Building the Chunking Name Wall

Review details about the physical construction, word cards, and affixing words to the Wall on pages 14 and 15. Then choose the pace for building your Wall: post the names all at once; do five to seven per day so you have your Wall up and going within a week; or post just a few each week as you highlight particular chunks. I prefer the first option, so right away, I can begin modeling making connections to the chunks in all the names we have available. Then, I simply highlight a few chunks each week for intense practice, following the same schedule I outlined in Chapter 3 for the basic letter-sound correspondences.

Organizing the Chunking Name Wall

Chunks, by definition, always begin with a vowel. Thus, I organize the chunking Name Wall in *a, e, i, o, u, y* and "other" categories (see Figure 5.1). The useful chunk in each name is underlined and fixed under the first vowel in the spelling of the rime. So, students' names containing a useful chunk beginning with the letter *a* are placed under the a category in either the long- or short-vowel column. For example, *Santos* would go under short *a* with the *an* chunk underlined; while *Shaday* would go under the long *a* with the *ay* chunk underlined.

Notice how the letter patterns we teach boldly stand out on your Wall when it's organized by vowels. I repeatedly point these generalizations out to students, and they become visually apparent as the Wall grows: "Look how we see so many of those long-vowel chunks ending in silent *e*," or "notice how many of those long-vowel chunks have two vowels together in the spelling. How does knowing these patterns help us as readers? How does knowing these patterns help us as spellers?"

We further make a point of reflecting on vowel generalizations when we post additional words beyond students' names:

Ms. Wag: We're adding the word *clap* to our Wall for the /ap/ chunk. Where should we post it?

Students: With the short-*a* chunks!

Ms. Wag: You've got it! Notice how *clap* is yet another short word with just one vowel and the vowel makes the short sound. We sure have added a lot of those to our short-vowel columns! What can we generalize about short vowels from all these words?

What about those chunks with variant vowel sounds? Omar's name could be used to highlight the *ar* chunk. But, it doesn't fit under long or short *a*. For rimes like these, I color the bottom of the foam board. *Omar* would still go under *a*, but way at the bottom of the board in this special, colored section. Students know this means, Yes, the chunk is spelled with the letter *a*, but it doesn't have the /a/ or /ā/ sound. The same is true for our placement of all chunks with variant vowels (like /ew/ in *Stewart*, /er/ in *Perla*, /oy/ in *Joy,* and /or/ in *Corey*). See Figure 5.1 to get a better idea of how this looks.

The y category works for names like *Mylee* and *Sherry* to represent sounds the letter *y* makes while acting as a vowel. You'll also have names without useful chunks. One year, I had two Zachs in my class. *Ack* is a great chunk for making many other words. But, the *a-c-h* spelling is unusual and you don't find it in words we read and write. *Naj* is another example of a name lacking a useful chunk for connecting to English words. Names like these are added to the Wall under the "other" heading. I explain to students,

> Names can be spelled many different ways. In fact, some are spelled in such unusual ways that the chunks inside them don't help us read and write other words. Let's take Zach's name. The /ack/ chunk is really helpful to us. Think of all the words with that sound. [*Share some of these among the class:* sack, rack, track, attack, backpack, *etc.*] But, /ack/ is never spelled *a-c-h* in those words. That's just the way /ack/ is spelled exclusively in Zach's name. So, we can't put Zach's name under the *a* chunks, since we wouldn't want to misspell all those words. But, we can put Zach's name under "other," since we can still use other parts

> **Note**
>
> *Many students' names contain highly frequent, incredibly useful chunks. For instance, the* an *and the* ay *chunks from Santos and Shaday's names appear on Edward Fry's (1998) list of the 38 most useful and frequently appearing rimes making up one-syllable words!*

inside it. Maybe, you're writing a word like *dizzy* and you think, I hear /zzzzz/ in the middle. I must need the letter *z* because I hear that same sound at the beginning of Zach's name. Or, maybe you hear the sound /a/ in a word you're writing and connect it to Zach's name to help you spell it. Similarly, names with foreign origins sometimes lack chunks that will help us with English words. I can't think of any words with the /aj/ chunk like in Naj's name. We'll put Naj's name under "other," too, because we can make other connections to it. You'll see, there are a lot of different ways to make connections from one word to another. When we learn to look at words and names flexibly, we find a lot of things in common!

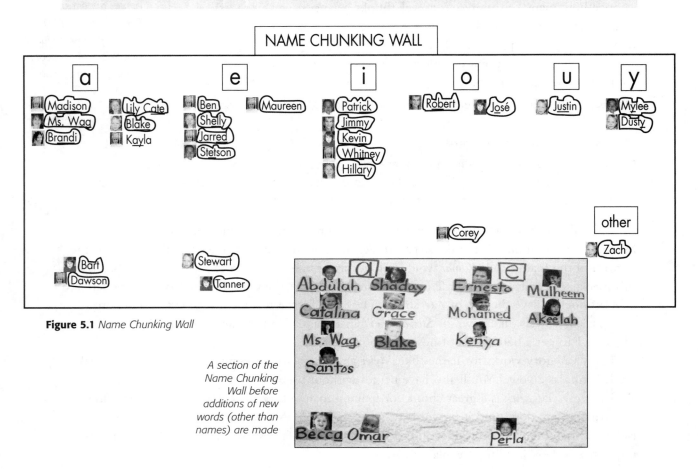

Figure 5.1 *Name Chunking Wall*

A section of the Name Chunking Wall before additions of new words (other than names) are made

Additionally, the "other" category comes in handy once we start posting additional words to our Wall to cover common word parts. I often post *tion*, *le*, and *ly* words since we use those syllables so often.

If you don't have names fitting all categories (*a, e, i, o, u, y,* and *other*), I suggest you still make these sections on your foam board for two reasons. First, you'll be using the same foam board from year to year. Over time, with different class rosters, you'll need all the categories. Second, as you'll see in "Extending the Chunking Name Wall to Include More Rimes," you'll need the sections to accommodate other words with useful chunks you want your students to learn beyond those in their names.

Why not organize the Chunking Name Wall in alphabetical order like the ABC Name Wall? The answer to this question comes down to ease of reference. With the ABC Name Wall, we are focusing on basic letter–sound correspondences and making most connections to beginning sounds. With chunks, we are focusing on a different part of the word. Since these word parts always start with a vowel, it makes sense to look for them under vowel headers. Imagine a student is reading along and becomes stuck on the word *milkshake*. If he sees the first syllable is *milk* but can't decode the last, his process might go something like this:

I see *milk*, but what is this part? I see the chunk starts with the letter *a*. Oh, yes, I see Blake's name under *a*. In *Blake, a-k-e* says /ake/. So, this must be milk . . . /sh/ /ake/ . . . *milkshake*.

By contrast, if *Blake* was fixed to the wall in alphabetical order, the student would have to scan the whole wall to find the *ake* chunk. Why would one look for *ake* under the letter *b*? The process is the same when locating words to aid spelling.

Pancake. Let's see . . . I know *p* then I hear /aaaaannnnn/. Oh yes, I know, *Santos*. I hear /an/ in *Santos* and it is spelled *a-n*. Now caaaaake. Let me see, under the *a* chunks . . . Oh! I see *Blake*, it has /aaaaake/ and it is spelled *a-k-e*. Both of those chunks help me spell *pancake*!

Again, it makes sense for these helpful word parts to be positioned under the corresponding vowel. As students segment words to hear the sounds to spell them, the vowel sound they hear will lead them to the proper place on the Wall for the reference they need. Naturally, students need a lot of guided practice to understand and apply this process. We'll look closely at that when we get into the Significant Lessons for Guided Spelling and Decoding at the Early/Developing Levels in Chapter 6.

One rule I stick to when building the Chunking Name Wall is to highlight only one chunk in multisyllabic names. This makes it easy to place the name on the Wall and find it to reference. Certainly, you can use other name parts that are not highlighted when reading or writing. If Charlie's name is under *a* with the *ar* chunk underlined, I might still demonstrate how to use the ending part of his name to help me figure out the last sound in an analogous word like cook*ie*.

Many names are multisyllabic, so they have more than one chunk. How do you know which chunk to choose? First, let's take a few names with chunks we've already mentioned: *Angie, Kayla, Mylee, Sherry,* and *Charlie*. *Angie* has the /an/ and the /ie/ chunks. Simply take each rime and test it to see how many analogous words you can generate. The chunk in the new word must have the same sound and spelling as the chunk in the name. /An/ is present in *tan, fan, man, sanity, banana, anchovy, dandelion, Stanley, candy, anecdote, ancestor, candidate, candlelight* . . .; the list goes on and on. Now, we'll do the same for the /ie/ chunk. *Cookie, frisbee, cutie* . . . I'm having a hard time coming up with others off the top of my head. Clearly, /an/ will be more helpful to my students in reading and writing new words. However, one other point to consider is names with duplicate chunks. If I have Angie in class along with Santos, and I'm already using *Santos* for /an/, then I may logically use *Angie* for the /ie/ chunk. *Charlie* also has the /ie/. But, with his name, I'd most likely use the /ar/ chunk since it is so frequent (see how many /ar/

words you can quickly come up with!). The logical choice for *Kayla* is the /ay/ chunk (again, test /ay/ versus /a/); but *Mylee* has two useful parts; the /y/ (*cry, sty, fly, shy, fry, by, try, why, spy, defy, verify, supply, clarify* . . .) and the /ee/ (*see, bee, tree, flee, spree, glee, fee, free, degree, filigree, chimpanzee* . . .). In cases like these, just pick one to highlight, realizing you can also refer to the other chunk when appropriate. *Sherry* is simple since the /er/ spelling in this name is irregularly pronounced (*a-i-r* and *a-r-e* are the common spellings). We're left with the /y/ chunk which is really useful (think of all the analogous words: *city, funny, sunny, dairy, phony, starry, cherry, fifty, gravy, daisy, delicacy, delivery, anthropology* . . .).

Now let's take *Samantha, Ignacio, Andrea, Tineka, Sidney, Skyler, Andy, Juan, Brett, Shane, Umberto, Abdulah,* and *Phillip*. What might you do with those names? Before reading on, take a second to test the chunks in each one. What might you conclude?

Let's start with the obvious ones: with *Samantha*, I'd go with /am/ or /an/ depending on the availability of either chunk in other names. I'd use /in/ for *Tineka*, /id/ from *Sidney*, /er/ from *Skyler*, /and/ from *Andy*, /ane/ from *Shane*, /um/ from *Umberto*, /ab/ from *Abdulah* and /ip/ from *Phillip*. All of these chunks make up many small and multisyllabic words. Interestingly, too, most have short-vowel sounds, which is the best place to start with younger or struggling students.

I'd underline /et/ in *Brett* and place it with the other short *e* chunks, explaining to students that most of the time, they'll see /et/ spelled *e-t* rather than *e-t-t* as in Brett's name. What about *Andrea*? Depends on the pronunciation. If it's pronounced "on -drea," we can't use the a-n spelling for /an/, so I'd place the name under "other." Naturally, if the *a-n* is pronounced /an/, I'd use it there. *Ignacio* is pretty simple since /ig/ is a nice chunk to work with. But what to do with *Juan*? Again, I'd explain to students how sometimes names don't have useful chunks for connecting to English words (as with the examples of *Zach* and *Naj* before), but we can use other parts of the name to help us in our reading and writing. *Juan* would go under the "other" category, since we might connect to the last sound in his name as we read and write /n/ words, for example.

Now, you try. List several of your current students' names off the top of your head. Go through and underline the chunks in each. Take a second to determine where the names may go on your Wall by quickly testing the chunks. Think about why you've made the decisions you have. Also, remember to give yourself enough professional leeway to try new things and make mistakes. If you place a name on the Wall in what you later deem to be the wrong place, just change it. When things like this happen in my classroom, I always make a big deal of them. I want students to see I make mistakes, too; that I try new things and reflect on what happens. This is a great learning experience for everyone!

Extending the Chunking Name Wall to Include More Rimes

There is no more effective way to introduce the idea of chunks and the analogy strategies than with students' names. Obviously, though, the chunks contained in your students' names each year are limited. There are always many additional chunks that provide lots of help for developing readers and writers (see Figure 5.2). So, how does one go about adding these to the Wall? Here are two options.

- You might add names of favorite characters from books, names of prominent people in your school, names of class pets or mascots, and so on. Add just one to use as your consistent reference for each chunk.

- Add one key word per chunk taken from a book, song, rhyme, poem, or chant. Since I already use songs, rhymes, poems, and chants for shared reading, then give kids copies for independent rereading, they make logical contexts for choosing additional words (this helps me integrate my curriculum).

Why post *just one* key word per chunk beyond those represented by your students' names? When you come back to *that same word* all year long, you're building in the repetition needed for mastery. That word gets stuck in students' memories. Plus, posting just one reference forces students to use the analogy strategies. If your Word Wall word is *fabulous* for the *ous* chunk, for example, students must think, "If I know *fabulous*, I spell *marvelous* like this" or, while reading, "This must be /ner/ /v/ . . . /ous/, like *fabulous!*" They'll use those strategies until the chunk becomes automatic.

> **Note**
>
> *Once we begin adding words other than names to our Wall, we simply refer to it as our "Chunking Wall."*

When might you begin extending your Wall beyond the chunks in students' names? I wait to begin this process until I feel most of the class has a firm grasp on how the analogy strategies work and they are using the chunks from the Wall. One way to check this is to turn the Wall around to the blank side and give a quiz. "I'll say a name from our Chunking Name Wall and I want you to write it and underline the chunk, spelling as accurately as you can." Depending on the grade level, as you give each name, you might also ask students to write some analogous words. "Now that you've written Kayla's name and underlined the chunk we use, please list any other words you know containing that chunk. Spell them the best you can." If you're pleased with how your students fared, noting many were able to correctly spell most chunks (though perhaps misspelling other parts of the names) and use them to logically generate other words, feel free to start extending your Wall. Keep in mind, you'll continue to refer to your students' names all year, even as you are adding new chunk-words, so there's plenty of time for more instruction and practice. (Remember, as discussed in the introduction of this book, I never retire words from Word Walls, so students who need more time to learn have the support they need.) If the quiz above is too difficult for your students, test only the most common chunks by saying the name, then asking students to just write the chunk.

Why use a "spelling quiz" to check students' understanding? Since reading and writing are so closely linked, and spelling abilities generally lag behind reading abilities (Blevins, 2006; Bear et al., 2007), you can be sure once students show they know something in spelling they've got it in reading. If students can hear the chunk in a name and spell it, they can decode it. You can certainly alter your assessment by making a reading list of the chunks already posted on your Wall for each child to independently read aloud to you. An alternative is to form a list of nonsense words (like made-up names) using chunks you've covered, beginning with short vowels first, then long. You might check out Pat Cunningham's (1990) "Names Test" for this purpose, as well (find it online with "Cunningham Name Test" in a search engine or review a recent adaptation in Mather, Sammons, & Schwartz, 2006).

Here are some general guidelines for adding non-name words to your Chunking Wall:

- **In kindergarten and with beginning English language learners:** Add just two words each week. Start with frequent, short-vowel chunks like /at/, /ip/, /am/, /ot/, /um/ and /et/. It's a good idea to post a picture cue next to each word to lend more support for emergent learners.

- **In first grade and with developing English language learners:** Add three words per week at first. Then, if you feel your students are doing well overall, increase your pace to four or five. As in kindergarten, it will be most beneficial to begin with simple short-vowel chunks and include picture cues.

- **In second grade:** Add five words each week. While I prefer using poems, songs, rhymes, and chants to find appropriate words, many teachers like posting a few key words from their weekly spelling list (of course, they pick those with the most useful chunks, testing them the same way we test names).

Naturally, these are just general guidelines and the best approach is to watch your learners closely and adjust your pace as necessary. For more information on working with words harvested from engaging literacy contexts, see my books *Teaching Reading and Writing With Word Walls* (1999) and *20 Weekly Word-Study Poetry Packets* (2003).

Again, take a moment to study how the generalizations we teach about vowels are so visually apparent on a more complete Chunking Wall (refer to Figure 5.2). Once you've added several words, you may want to remove everything, re-sort via vowel pattern (i.e., *a* chunks spelled with silent *e*; *a* chunks spelled with double vowels), and re-post to emphasize the generalizations.

Introducing the Chunking Name Wall

Here's how I introduce the Chunking Name Wall to developing English language learners and at the beginning of the second-grade school year (see the notes below for the beginning English language learners, kindergarten/first-grade introduction):

Boys and girls, what do you do when you come to a word you don't know in your reading?
    [*Students reply, "Sound it out!"*]
Can anyone tell me more about that? How do you sound it out?
    [*Students often say something like, "You look at the letters and think of the sounds they make."*]

NAME CHUNKING WALL

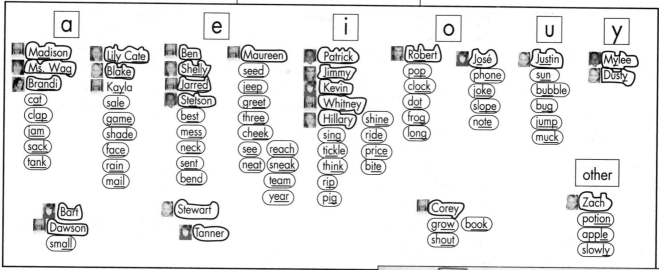

a		e		i		o		u	y

a
- Madison
- Ms. Wag
- Brandi
- cat
- clap
- jam
- sack
- tank

- Lily Cate
- Blake
- Kayla
- sale
- game
- shade
- face
- rain
- mail

- Bart
- Dawson
- small

e
- Ben
- Shelly
- Jarred
- Stetson
- best
- mess
- neck
- sent
- bend

- Maureen
- seed
- jeep
- greet
- three
- cheek
- see   reach
- neat   sneak
- team
- year

- Stewart
- Tanner

i
- Patrick
- Jimmy
- Kevin
- Whitney
- Hillary   shine
- sing   ride
- tickle   price
- think   bite
- rip
- pig

o
- Robert
- pop
- clock
- dot
- frog
- long

- José
- phone
- joke
- slope
- note

- Corey
- grow   book
- shout

u
- Justin
- sun
- bubble
- bug
- jump
- muck

y
- Mylee
- Dusty

other
- Zach
- potion
- apple
- slowly

Figure 5.2 *Chunking Wall with additions of words beyond students' names*

Okay. Let me show you a big, long last name and we'll talk about sounding it out. Don't say it out loud, even if you figure it out, until I tell you to do so. Here's the word [*writing on the whiteboard*]: *Randettervick*. [*I make up a name using chunks from students' names.*] When you see a word you don't know, do you sound it out like this [*using a piece of cardstock to cover all but one letter at a time moving from left to right*]: /r/ /a/ /n/ /d/ /e/ /t/ /t/ /e/ /r/ /v/ /i/ /c/ /k/? Is that what you mean?

[*Some students respond yes, others no, and some don't respond at all.*]

Sounding out letter-by-letter is one way of looking at words. As you've gotten to know the letters of the alphabet, you probably learned to look at words that way. But the sounds individual letters make can be different from word to word, and once you figure out each sound, it can be hard to blend them together to actually read the word. Let me show you another way to look at words. I'm going to look inside this word for groups of letters that hang out together. We call these *chunks*. The chunks have the same sound from word to word and they are easy to blend together. Watch [*using the cardstock to cover the whole word, uncovering one syllable at a time, moving from left to right*]: /Rand/ /et/ /ter/ /vick/, [*blending*] Randettervick! I see /and/ like in Brandi's name, so the first part is /rrrrr and/ and [*placing Brandi's name card above* Rand *on the board using sticky tack*]. I see /et/ like in Stetson's name [*placing Stetson's name card above* et]. Then, I see /er/ like in Perla's name, so this must be /ttttt er/ [*showing Perla's card*] and I see /ick/ like in Patrick's name, so this must be /vvvvv ick/ [*showing Patrick's card*]. Randettervick! Does that seem easier than /r/ /a/ /n/ /d/ /e/ /t/ /t/ /e/ /r/ /v/ /i/ /c/ /k/?

[*Students exclaim, "Yes!"*]

That's why we are building the Chunking Name Wall. Our classmates' names have great chunks we can use to read and write lots of words. Some names even have more than one useful chunk, like /P at r ick/! I'll show you how to use the chunks when I read and write words and we'll practice together. Each week, we'll focus on learning a few of the chunks on our Wall. This will help us read and write new words more easily than ever before! Once we get to know and are using the chunks in our names, we'll add other words with good chunks to our Chunking Wall. You can still use what you already know about words, like sounding out letters one by one when you're stuck, but we'll add using chunks to your good-reader strategies.

You'll find the chunks will help you the same way in your writing. Rather than stretching a word you're trying to spell into its tiniest sounds, I'll teach you to listen for the chunks, then use the names you know to spell those chunks. Watch. If I'm trying to spell the word *filling*, I can use Hillary's name to spell the first chunk [*holding up Hillary's name card and writing on the board*]. If this is /Hill ary/, then I must need /fffff/, the letter *f*, and *i-l-l* for the /ill/ chunk: /f ill/. Then I know /ing/ by heart because it's in so many other words, *i-n-g*. That was easy! Once I know the chunks, I can use them to spell many words!

Let's take just a minute to look at some of our names and play with their chunks. [*I hold up several name cards, one by one, read the name, and voice the chunk.*] Here we have Mohamed's name. His name has three syllables or beats—/Mo/ /ha/ /med/—and we see the /ed/ chunk underlined on his name card. Help me think of some words with the /ed/ chunk so you can see how it will be helpful for reading and writing.

[*Students call out words such as* bed, Ted, red, fed, wed, led.]

Yep! Think of bigger words too, like *wedding, medicine, education*. Try different beginning sounds, add the /ed/ chunk and see what you get.

[*I continue generating /ed/ words aloud, pushing for words with complex onsets and multiple syllables. Then, I show another name card, break the name into syllables* and play with the underlined chunk in that name. We continue working with names and chunks from the Chunking Name Wall, then close the lesson.*] Wow! We just came up with a lot of words using the chunks in some of our names. See why we're building the Chunking Name Wall? We can use the names on the Wall to help us spell chunks in words we're writing and figure out chunks in words we're reading. Over time, we'll get to know the chunks by heart and become really comfortable using the chunking strategy to read and write new words.

* Use the concrete models from Chapter 1 to help students clearly understand syllables.

Follow the introduction with lots of teacher modeling. When you write on the board, break words into syllables and chunks, and think aloud using the names on your Wall to spell. Do the same as you're reading aloud or engaged in shared reading. Constant modeling will go a long way toward helping your students understand the analogy strategies and how to use the Name Wall.

With Beginning English Language Learners and in Kindergarten and First Grade

The introduction to chunking includes a bow to the work we've already done with names and the reassurance the ABC Name Wall will continue to be used and available for support. Then, my lesson follows the same general plan. I tell students we'll learn another way to look at words by noticing chunks (groups of letters that hang together and are the same from word to word). As in the second-grade example, I write a last name on the board that contains chunks from students' names; but one that is developmentally appropriate such as *Mander* or *Lobin* (shorter name, simple onsets, short-vowel chunks). Next, we orally generate analogous words for the chunks in several kids' names, then close the lesson with our overall purpose for building and using the Wall.

Pacing

Just as I suggested with the ABC Name Wall, it's important to focus on and practice a few chunks each week, thus building familiarity and automaticity. And, just as with the ABC Name Wall, this doesn't mean every child will have mastered the chunks when the week is done. With the support of the Chunking Name Wall, that happens over time.

Here's the weekly schedule I use for working with names on the Wall. You'll notice it's identical to the ABC Name Wall schedule:

Monday: Pick the focus chunks (again, two for K and beginning ELLs; three—building to four or five, if desired—for first grade and developing ELLs; five for second grade).

Introduce the names and chunks (or reintroduce if they were already posted).

Tues.–Fri.: Practice these intensively throughout the week (See "Differentiated Practice Activities," page 94).

Friday: Post (or re-post) the names on the Chunking Wall.

Use, use, use the names and chunks to read and write new words in multiple contexts for the rest of the school year! (See "Significant Lessons for Guided Spelling and Guided Decoding" in Chapter 6.)

Beginning Each Week

If, as I do, you post all the names at once, remove the key name cards of the week from your Wall on Monday, tacking them with sticky tack to your front-and-center chalkboard or whiteboard. Use concrete

> ### Helpful Hint
>
> *An effective way to introduce the concept of chunking to young or less experienced children in general is to focus on a chunk most know already: /ing/. I take digital photos of students doing things around the classroom (building with blocks, cleaning the sink, sharpening a pencil, etc.) then put them into a class book (see Real-e Books, page 62). The students' names are in the text and I underline the /ing/ chunk in the words. We read the book again and again, reviewing how that i-n-g chunk sounds the same and is spelled the same in all those words on every page.*

> ### Note
>
> *If you have a traditional spelling program with a weekly list: Add the names with the chunks of the week to the list (or, if that doesn't seem appropriate [when the spellings of the names are too difficult or unusual], add a few words with the chunks).*

models to segment the names into phonemes and syllables, then call attention to the sound and spelling of the chunk you've underlined. Work with the class to orally generate analogous words, discussing how the chunk in the name will be helpful to you as readers and writers.

This week, we'll be working with the /an/ chunk in Stanley's name, the /it/ chunk in Takitja's name, the /er/ chunk in Tanner's name and the /im/ chunk in Kimberly's name [*pointing to each name card in turn*]. You know names are made up of sounds, right? Let's take Kimberly's name. If we say her name slowly, listening inside it, we can stretch it to hear all the sounds: /Kkkkk/ /iiiii/ /mmmmm/ /bbbbb/ /errrrr/ /lllll/ /yyyyy/. [*I show the slinky or elastic-band model as described in Chapter 1.*] We can also break her name into the big word parts—the syllables or beats. Try that with me [*using the elastic syllable model*]: /Kim/ /ber/ /ly/ [*clapping*]. /Kim/ /ber/ /ly/ [*feeling our jaws drop*]. /Kim/ /ber/ /ly/ [*humming*]. [*For information on using these techniques to detect syllables, see page 23*].

As you can see and hear, her name has three syllables and three chunks. The chunks are the vowel and what comes after in each syllable. The first chunk in Kimberly's name is a great one to use to read and write new words: /im/ [*showing Kimberly's name card with the /im/ underlined*]. Say *Kimberly* with me again, listening to hear the /im/ chunk [*we repeat /Kim/ /ber/ /ly/*]. Can you hear it? Where is it in her name? [*Using the elastic syllable model*]: the first syllable [*voicing /Kim/, lips under the first piece of cardstock*], the second syllable [*voicing /ber/*], or the third [*voicing /ly/*]?

Figure 5.3 *I use the elastic model to show and discuss the syllables in Kimberly's name. Here, the mouth position at the end of the first syllable is emphasized.*

If children have trouble identifying the chunk, have them focus on their mouth position as described in previous chapters.

Yes, the first. [*I segment and blend /Kim/ /ber/ /ly/ again, using the elastic model.*] The /im/ chunk is spelled *i-m*. Did you also notice that the second chunk /er/ is the same chunk we are highlighting in Tanner's name? See? These chunks are common and occur in many words! That's why we're learning to use them!

Can you think of many words that have the /im/ chunk from Kimberly's name? [*After wait-time*] Turn to your neighbor and share. [*I listen in so I can repeat examples.*] I heard *him, slim, rim, skim, trim, himself*. . . . Remember to try for some longer words, too, like *chimney, shimmering, whimper, criminal*. . . . These are all words that have /im/. The chunk is spelled the same *i-m* in all of them! So, if you know Kimberly's name you can use it to help you spell or read the /im/ chunk inside these words. Check out this word. [*I write* impossible *on the board.*] Do you see the /im/ chunk? It's the first chunk in this big word: /im/ /poss/ /ib/ /le/, impossible! See how the chunks in our names will be helpful to us? That's why we're building our Chunking Name Wall. We'll be able to use it all year, really getting to know these word parts and how to use them well. Let's look at another name we're focusing on this week.

As the lesson continues, segment and blend phonemes and syllables in the other names of the week using models. Identify each focus chunk and orally generate analogous words so students see the utility of the chunks. Then provide some form of guided practice in identifying these target chunks, as with the sound boards below.

Guided Practice: Sound Boards

I use Sound Boards as one option for guided practice when we're first practicing new chunks at the beginning of the week. You can guide students to hear and match chunks orally only or extend the lesson to involve phonics practice. When using Sound Boards to focus on chunks, we work in exactly the same manner as we do for phonemes or letter sounds (see "Sound Boards" in Chapters 3 and 4): Student photos are at the top of the columns. I say words containing the key chunks in the names. Students repeat the words, testing the names on the board for a match. They place a marker in the column to indicate where they hear the match. We discuss each example, analyzing challenging ones with concrete models. Keep in mind, the more difficult the words are to match (complex onsets, multiple syllables, unusual vocabulary), the more difficult the activity, so adjust accordingly. Here's a very brief review:

> Your word to match is *brittle*. Have you ever had peanut brittle? Repeat the word, *brittle*. Whose name has a matching chunk? [*Guide students to hear the syllables in the word, then identify the chunks. A marker goes in Takitja's column as her name shares the /it/ chunk with* brittle.] So, if I was spelling *brittle*, the /it/ chunk would be spelled *i-t*, just like in *Takitja*.

Again, guide students to feel how the chunk is made in their mouths, if appropriate. Then give them another word to test and match.

Extending the Lesson

Students *write* analogous words in the Sound Board columns using a word bank or word cards in a center, or working with a partner to hunt for words (once students are more experienced, or for those who need more challenge). Again, provide simple, single-syllable words for your students to match or more difficult words, as appropriate.

When students need a lot of support for success you can

- fold back one or two columns to modify the Sound Board, then work with them in small groups, matching words orally with the assistance of concrete models (see Figure 5.5);

Figure 5.4 *Second Grade Sound Board featuring Stanley, Takitja, Tanner, and Kimberly. Higher-level students generated analogous words using the chunks in the names.*

- share the pencil to write words; or
- make an overhead transparency of the Sound Board and work together to write words in columns using a word bank.

Be sure to see "Sound Boards" in Chapter 2 (page 36) for detailed differentiated practice ideas. Writing analogous words on the Sound Boards also makes a great take-home activity.

Figure 5.5 *Modified Sound Board (one column is folded under to make the task easier) used in small group to match chunks orally using Cheerios as markers*

Throughout the Week: Differentiated Practice Activities

Building automaticity with chunks is key to reading and writing fluency. Students who master spelling patterns don't have to take time to make Word Wall connections. The more efficiently they can decode, the less time they spend on word-level processing, freeing up more mental energy for comprehension. The same is true for writing. When spelling is more automatic, writers can focus on higher-level processes. Be sure students know why these lessons are important. Good readers and writers know a lot of chunks since having them in their heads makes reading and writing easier!

These lessons support strategic knowledge as well, since they show students how chunks in names connect to chunks in other words. For example, they learn: "If I can read *Shaday*, then I can read *ray, stay,* and *playground*." "If I can spell *Justin*, then I can spell *must, crust,* and *trusting*."

Practice Pages

Practice Pages are designed to promote spelling and decoding by analogy while building automaticity. Names and chunks are listed on the left side of the page with space for students to write analogous words in between. Student photos are on the right quarter of the page to provide cues for rereading or self-checking. These are folded under on the dotted line when in use.

When I hand out the blank page, we read each name, spell it, voice the chunk, spell it aloud, and trace it. (If students are new to Practice Pages, make a transparency so you can easily model.)

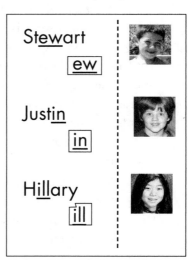

Figure 5.6 *Practice Page for spelling and decoding by analogy*

Next, we come up with three or four analogous words to record directly under the name. The matching chunk in each word is underlined.

Ms. Wag: The first name on our Practice Page is *Stewart* with the /ew/ chunk. If you know how to spell /ew/ in *Stewart*, what other words can you spell? Let's start with an easy one.

Student: *New* is like *Stewart*.

Ms. Wag: Great! So, how will *new* be spelled?

All: *N-e-w!*

Ms. Wag: [*Writing it on my page*] Yep! If this is /Stew/, *e-w*, then this is *new*, *n-e-w*. The chunk stays the same. Underline /ew/ and make sure you spelled it correctly on your Practice Page. Okay, who has a more challenging /ew/ word?

Student: *Crew!*

Ms. Wag: Okay, like the crew of workers or group of workers on a ship. Crew. If this is /Stew/ [*running my finger under the syllable*], then what will you have for *crew*?

Student: *K-r-e-w.*

Student: No, *c-r-e-w!*

Ms. Wag: Which is correct? [*Writing both spellings on the board*]

Students: *C-r-e-w.*

Ms. Wag: Yes, sometimes you have to try a word more than once and step back and look at it to see which spelling looks right. It could be *k-r-e-w*, since *k-r* says /cr/ like in the word *krill*. But, in the word *crew*, it is spelled *c-r*, and most /cr/ words are spelled *c-r*, not *k-r*. Good job keeping the chunk the same, *e-w* /ew/. Did you underline it? So, we have *c-r-e-w* [*writing it on my page*]. Now, let's try one more even harder word.

Student: *Chewing.*

Ms. Wag: There's a two-syllable word. Chunk it and give it a try. [*Wait-time*] What do you think? Let's try the first syllable, *chew*. If this is /Stew/ [*running my finger under the syllable*], then how will we spell *chew*?

All: *C-h-e-w*!

Ms. Wag: Yep, *c-h*, just like Charlie's name on our Wall and *e-w* like *Stewart*. Now, the /ing/ chunk is easy; it's in so many words! How do we spell that chunk?

All: *i-n-g*!

Ms. Wag: You've got it. Now make sure you wrote it correctly on your Practice Page so when you go back to reread it, you can. *C-h-e-w-i-n-g* [*writing on my page*]. Let's reread what we came up with for the /ew/ chunk in *Stewart*. If this is *Stewart* [*running my finger under the name*], then this is— read with me, class—

All: *New, crew, chewing*!

Ms. Wag: Super. Let's go on to the next name on our Practice Page: *Justin* with the /ust/ chunk. Let's start with a simple /ust/ word. Anybody think of one?

The class (or group) works together to fill in the rest of the Practice Page (see Figure 5.7). Upon finishing, we fold the photo clues back on the dotted line and try to read the whole page without looking at the clues (the photo helps students who are stuck read the key name and chunk, thus also providing them help to read the analogous words). We then add the page to our "Practice Folder" (a two-pocket folder) where previously completed pages are kept. I give the students three or four minutes to reread the pages in their folders once or twice a week. They love testing themselves to see if they can read quickly without looking at the photo clues. This is easy, effective practice!

Lesson Notes

Make the lesson multilevel by starting with easier words to write before getting into harder words (with complex onsets and multiple syllables). This way, you're meeting the needs of more students.

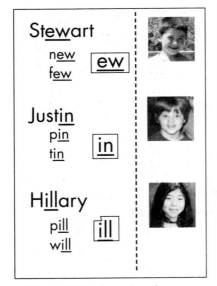

Figure 5.7 *Simple version of Practice Page*

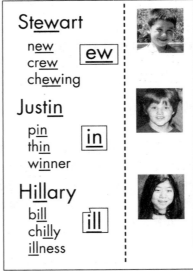

Figure 5.8 *More challenging version of Practice Page*

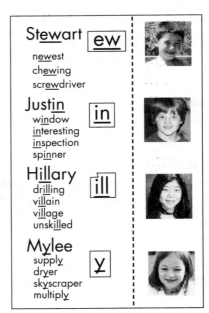

Figure 5.9 *Most challenging version of Practice Page*

Differentiating Practice Pages

Remember, too, this lesson lends itself to multiple grouping configurations. Your lowest group, for example, may meet to record just one or two simple, single-syllable analogous words for each key name and chunk (see Figure 5.8). If this is still too difficult, you can cut away the last name and chunk so they have fewer to work with. In any case, by differentiating the task, the words they are spelling and rereading from their pages are just right for their needs.

Your above-level group may add only more difficult, multisyllabic words, and even work with an additional name and chunk. (I simply cut the last name and photo off the page before I hand it out to other groups; see Figure 5.9.)

Read Some/Write Some

Read Some/Write Some is a quick way to practice using the chunks of the week to read and write new words. It focuses on direct application and promotes positive transfer of patterns into students' independent reading and writing. It's easier than the lessons that require students to make connections while referring to *all* the words on the Wall (Chapter 6). Let's say this week in first grade, we're focusing on *Ahnim, Nadira, Scott,* and *Brooke* (the /im/, /ad/, /ot/, and /ook/ rimes).

Ms. Wag: I'm going to ask you to read some words that have the chunks we're focusing on this week. You'll see how these names: *Ahnim, Nadira, Scott,* and *Brooke* and these chunks: /im/, /ad/, /ot/, and /ook/ will be really helpful to you as readers. Let's try one. Remember to wait for five fingers so everyone has a chance to give the word a try. [*See page 67 for the "Five Finger Rule."*]

I start with simple words and progressively increase the difficulty. Writing *look* on the whiteboard, I slowly hold up five fingers, one at a time.

Students: *Look*!

Ms. Wag: The word is *look*, just like which name from our Wall?

Students: *Brooke*!

Ms. Wag: So, if I'm reading along and come to this word, I may think, *If I know* Brooke [*holding Brooke's name card just above the word* look *on the board*], this is /llll ook/. [*Next, I write* rotten *on the board, thus incorporating two simple syllables, and slowly hold up five fingers.*]

Students: *Rotten*!

Ms. Wag: *Rotten*! How did you know this word is *rotten*? Who can tell me how they figured out this word?

Student: I used the chunk in Scott's name and I sounded it out /rot/ /ten/.

Ms. Wag: So, if I know *Scott* [*holding the name card* Sc<u>ott</u> *above the word* rotten *on the board*], this is /rot/ and /ten/. The /en/ chunk is in Ben's name! Or, maybe you know the word *ten* already, so it was easy, /rot/ /ten/!"

Student: How about *robot*?

Ms. Wag: You're right! If you know *Scott*, you can also read *robot* [*writing* robot *on the board*]. Great job, readers! Okay, here's another one. [*I write* gladly *on the board and review decoding strategies while holding up five fingers.*]

Ms. Wag: Look at the parts: the beginning sounds and chunks. Look for a name with a matching chunk, beginning with the same vowel.

Students: *Gladly*!

Ms. Wag: That's it! /Gl ad ly/. Which name helped us?

Students: *Nadira*!

Ms. Wag: If we know *Nadira*, the /ad/ chunk [*holding the name card* N͟adira *just above the word*], we can read, /gl/ /ad/ /ly/. We see *l-y* at the end of many words, right? Now, let's pass out the whiteboards and we'll try to *write* some words with these chunks.

Ms. Wag: [*After dispersing materials*] Let's try a simple one first. How about the word *slim*, like, *I have a slim chance of winning the race*. What would you do as a speller to write *slim*?

Student: Say the word and listen for the beginning sounds and chunk.

Ms. Wag: Good thinking. Once you hear the chunk, think of other words that have that same chunk and if you need to, look at the word card to spell it. Okay, spellers, try it on your boards! [*After wait-time*] Hold up your boards. Wow! I see it spelled correctly! How did you do that?

Student: It has the /im/ chunk!

Ms. Wag: Yep, it has the /im/ chunk just like in *Ahnim* [*holding up the name card*]. And, the chunk is spelled the same way *i-m*. The spelling stays the same from word to word. Ahnim's name will be on the Name Wall all year under the *i* chunks to help you learn the spelling. Let's try another word. How about *cooking*, like, *Dad was cooking dinner*. Give *cooking* a try on your boards. [*After wait-time*] Hold up your boards. Who wants to tell us how they spelled *cooking*?

Student: Cook has /ook/ like in Brooke's name and the /ing/ is easy.

Ms. Wag: Why is the /ing/ so easy?

Students: Because it's in so many words!

Ms. Wag: Wow! That's what great readers and writers do. They notice the letters that hang together across lots of words. They know these chunks by heart! Good job with *cooking*, class. If I know *Catalina*, I know *c* and, if I know *Brooke*, I spell /ook/ *o-o-k*. The /ing/ *i-n-g* is easy, I know it by heart from lots of other words. Here's our last word to try. It's a harder one: *otter*.

> ### Note
>
> *Though the /ot/ and /ook/ chunks are spelled with one extra letter in* Scott *and* Brooke, *we can highlight the common spelling of the rime on the name card for the Wall. We did the same with /et/ in the name* Brett *at the beginning of the chapter. Simply explain, "Though the /ot/ chunk is spelled o-t-t in Scott's name, you'll see it spelled o-t in the words you're reading and you'll need to spell it o-t in the words you're writing. Names often have unique spellings. We have to practice the most common way we'll see and spell /ot/ so we give our brains good practice. It's great that Scott's name has this useful chunk in it!"*

We work through *otter* in a similar manner.

Remember to adjust the lesson difficulty, have students read some and write some with simple, single-syllable words in kindergarten and more complex onsets and more syllables in second grade.

Chunk Races

"Ready? 30 seconds! Go!" These are familiar words for my students. They love to race against the clock to see how many times they can write a chunk. First, they write a key name of the week with the chunk underlined at the top of their whiteboards. I emphasize correctness, exclaiming, "Make sure you write it correctly! You don't want to give your brain bad practice!" Then, they race for 30 seconds, recording the chunk over and over, count their total, then race for another 30 seconds, trying to beat their last tally. It's that simple! Chunk Races build automaticity with chunks and are another easy transition activity kids really enjoy. Be sure to remind them they're racing with chunks to help them quickly and easily spell and read new words. Generate a few analogous words aloud to reinforce the idea.

Name Sort

Using your computer, type the key names of the week in bold font (36-point) with the chunks underlined at the top of a page. Then generate a one-page list of words containing the chunks in smaller font. Start with easy, one-syllable, analogous words with simple onsets. Format the words in columns. As you move down the page, add more and more complex words. Print a copy for each student.

Differentiate practice when you distribute the page: struggling readers get only the top 1/3 of the page to sort (containing the easiest analogous words); on-level readers get 2/3 of the page; and above-level readers get the whole page.

When students get their copies, they cut from the bottom of the page up the columns, then across to make little word cards to sort. They sort them on the floor or on their desks. A word must be read aloud before it is sorted under the key name. When complete, students check with a buddy, gather their word cards, and place them in an envelope to take home. If they redo the sort at home, they bring back the envelope with a signature and I award them an extra-credit point.

If you find you have readers that need even more challenge, include more words to sort and multisyllabic, harder vocabulary near the bottom; see Figure 5.11. Differentiate practice by cutting the page into sections as before, but this time you may need four portions, reserving the last one for your most advanced students.

For more emergent students, stick with just two key names and chunks at the top and list simple words in extra large font throughout. Keep it manageable by including just two columns of words to sort.

Lily Cate Dawson	Whitney	
saw	ate	it
late	sit	paw
jaw	gate	sit
bit	raw	hate
fit	draw	mit
claw	mate	date
plate	hit	flaw
slaw	spit	skit
state	drawing	skate
itself	seesaw	kitten
skater	mittens	straws

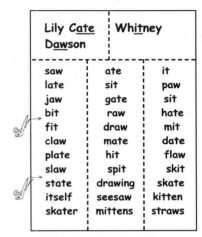

Figure 5.10 *Name Sort for on-level readers*

Lily Cate	Whitney	Dawson	
saw	ate	it	late
gate	sit	jaw	paw
bit	raw	hate	fit
draw	mit	claw	mate
date	plate	hit	flaw
slaw	spit	skit	state
skate	grit	grate	straws
slate	seesaw	mitten	itself
drawing	hated	later	awful
written	coleslaw	inflate	Hobbit
flawless	debate	awesome	knitting
brittle	critters	hesitate	
investigate	jawbreaker	witnesses	

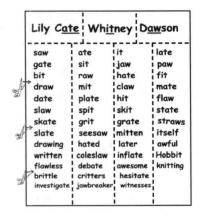

Figure 5.11 *Name Sort for above-level readers*

Cloze Morning Message With Blanks

Students put their heads together with their teammates to determine which chunks of the week belong in the blanks in words in the morning message; see Figure 5.12. To do this, they must integrate reading cues (What fits here? What would make sense?), reading strategies (reading on, rereading), and connect to our key

Dear Cla___ ,

Tod__ we'll have a special vis__or. She has writt__ lots of poetr_. She'll share some secr__s for writing good poems. After list__ing, we'll g__ to try writing our own poems. I b__ you'll love __!

Sincerely,
Ms. Wag.

Figure 5.12 *Cloze morning message with blanks*

names. Plus, they see how useful these chunks really are! As we study more and more chunks, I incorporate these into the Morning Message, as well.

(See details about different Morning Message variations and using the Numbered Heads Together technique on page 54.)

Singing the Chunks

Use this fun tune (adapted from *I Like the Rain* [Belanger, 1988]) to review the chunks of the week. Your students won't want to stop after just this week's names, so be prepared for even more review!

We know <u>Blake</u>,
We know /<u>ake</u>/.
How do you spell it?
<u>a-k-e</u> (clap)
We know /<u>ake</u>/.

We know <u>Briell</u>,
We know /<u>ell</u>/.
How do you spell it?
<u>e-l-l</u> (clap)
We know /<u>ell</u>/.

We know <u>Enrique</u>,
We know /<u>en</u>/.
How do you spell it?
<u>e-n</u> (clap, clap)
We know /<u>en</u>/.

Figure 5.13 *Music for singing the chunks*

Word Hunts

Divide a piece of chart paper or poster board into columns, one for each chunk of the week. Volunteers add to the charts when they encounter an analogous word. Review the list a few times during the week, encouraging students to hunt for words in any of their reading and writing (even at home),
discussing new vocabulary, adding to spelling dictionaries, and so on. Who can come up with the longest word containing a chunk of the week? The most unusual word? Next Monday, put up a new poster to start a new Word Hunt.

> **Variation**
>
> **Word Treasure**
> *Make a poster-size picture of a treasure chest. Laminate it. As students find words with the chunks of the week, they write them on the treasure chest with a dry-erase marker. Key names of the week are written on the lid with the chunks underlined.*

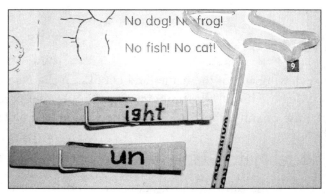

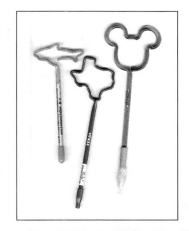

Figure 5.14 *Various highlighting tools*

Unique Highlighting Ideas

Write the chunks of the week on wooden clothespins. If you come across a chunk during shared reading of big books or charts, attach the clothespin to the page or line on the chart where it was found. Leave it there until you come across the chunk again, then move the clothespin. This encourages students to always be on the lookout for these key rimes, since they love to be the person who moves the clothespin!

Use highlighting tape to highlight chunks in big books, on posters, and so on. Instead of purchasing expensive highlighting tape in tape dispensers, look for "book cover" in store office supply sections. It's packaged in rolls like contact paper (it's transparent adhesive material), comes in assorted bright colors, can be cut to any size, is easy-on, easy-off, and it's cheap! It's most easily found during back-to-school time, since older students use it to cover their textbooks. There's so much material on each roll, a few rolls will last your whole teaching career!

When using overhead transparencies for shared reading, use plastic shape pen or pencil toppers to frame words with key chunks in "windows." Students love to do this in a poem/rhyme/chant overhead center, too!

Want More?

Several of the activities outlined in Chapter 3, though described there for basic letter sounds, will also work for reviewing the chunks of the week. For example, adapt "Read, Match, & Write" by labeling the middle column "chunk"; do "Name-o" having students rainbow write and underline the chunks during each round; and alter "Letter Search" to "Chunk Search."

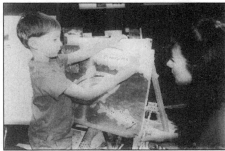

Figure 5.15 *Highlighting words in a big book*

Figure 5.16 *A roll of book cover material I use as highlighting tape*

Read <u>Brandi</u>	Chunk <u>and</u>	Write <u>and</u>
St<u>et</u>son	et	<u>et</u>
D<u>aw</u>son	aw	<u>aw</u>

Figure 5.17 *Read, Match, & Write with chunks*

Anytime Activities

These activities are useful for reviewing any of the names and chunks on the Name Wall, rather than those specific to the week. See the list of "Anytime Activities" in Chapter 3, substituting the use of chunks for letters, for a host of other useful ideas.

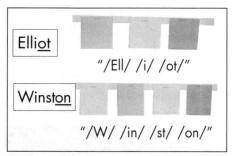

Figure 5.18 *Model Match-Up with Name Cards to work on phonological awareness of chunks and onsets and rimes*

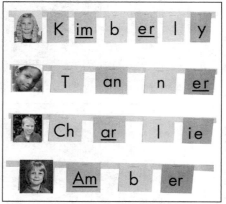

Figure 5.19 *Model Match-Up with photos to work on segmenting and blending*

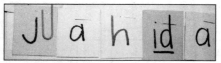

Figure 5.20 *A variation of Model Match-Up, where the photo clue is hidden by folding it over with a paper clip*

Figure 5.21 *A favorite variation of Model Match-Up*

Model Match-Up

Match name cards to various concrete models to reinforce chunking. Once a match is made, students must segment and blend three times using the model.

The name card *Elliot* is matched with an elastic model showing three chunks, while Winston's name card is matched with an elastic model depicting the onsets and rimes making up the name. (See Figure 5.18.)

Program models to specific students by stapling a photo on the elastic with the name written on cardstock pieces (representing each onset and rime as in Figure 5.19). Children read the name, then segment and blend the onsets and rimes three times. Have parent volunteers make them for your class. Just give them an example and list of names as you'd like them represented.

Make models for key words you'll use from year to year (think about grade- and content-specific vocabulary you always study, for example). When adding a picture clue, staple on a sticker or magazine cutout. Use them for the above activities.

Chant, Clap, Write

This activity also promotes automaticity with chunks and is a great way to review the Name Wall. A volunteer points to a name on the Wall (using a laser pointer adds an element of fun). The class chants the name, claps the spelling, then quickly writes the chunk on scratch paper. Within seconds, we're off to the next name! After we've done a few, a new volunteer comes forward to lead. Keep the pace swift and students will love it! (See Variations on page 103.)

Variation

Use a paper clip to hide the photo clue. Read the name, segment and blend, self-check by peeking at the picture. (See Figure 5.20.)

A Favorite

Match a name card to a model. Then think of analogous words that would also fit the model. Record your results on paper. (See Figure 5.21.)

Name Card Fold-Overs

Hold up one name card at a time from your large font (100-point) set, while folding the end of the name over the front, masking all but the beginning sound. (See Figure 5.22.) Students predict the name, then check with the chunks as they are unmasked. Be sure to turn the Name Wall around to the blank side, so students can't see the name cards and photos. Once they're adept at predicting, cross-checking, and reading first names, do the same with last names.

Figure 5.22 *Name Card Fold-Overs*

Onset and Rime Match-Up

Using one set of large font name cards, cut names into onsets and rimes. Place the cards in a center for students to match up. If you have a large class, put half, a third, or a fourth of the set into separate envelopes, so students have fewer pieces to work with at one time. Put a list of the names included in each envelope on the inside to support students having difficulty and for self-checking. Extend the activity: once matches are made, students mix the pieces, trying to match up any onset with any rime to make a real word. These are recorded on paper. (See Figure 5.23.)

For example, in one envelope you have a list of the names, *Blake, Samantha, Robert, Shelly, Patrick,* and letter cards representing their onsets and rimes: *Bl, ake; S, a, m, an, th, a; R, ob, ert, Sh, ell, y; P, at, r, ick.* After matching the pieces to make the names (self-checking the list), a student might then use the word parts to make and record such words as *sake, rake, shake; Rick, sick, pick, thick;* and *throb, rob, sob, blob.* Try this yourself using some of your students' names. It's a fun challenge!

Variations

Any Word Wall cheer can be extended to include quickly writing the chunk after each name. My students love the movement involved in standing cheers or partner cheers. Once they've cheered the name, they quickly take their seats to record the chunk, then pop back up again!

Here's a fun partner cheer: *Chant the name, stand and lightly bump fists with a buddy as it's spelled, return to seat, write the chunk, pop back up to buddy position.*

Hint

Search the Internet for Word Wall Cheers to find all kinds of ideas!

Variation

An easier version: *just cut the beginning onset in the name away from the rest. Students must match only two pieces to remake the names. (See Figure 5.24.)*

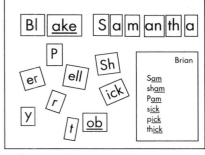

Figure 5.23 *Onset and Rime Match-Up with student-generated words*

Word Ladders

Given a classmate's name, how high can you build your word ladder in two minutes (climbing up a page writing words by association; see Figure 5.25)? For example, if we start with the name *Justin*, a word ladder may go:

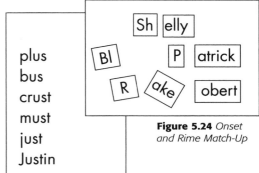

Figure 5.24 *Onset and Rime Match-Up*

plus
bus
crust
must
just
Justin

Figure 5.25 *Word Ladder*

I know *Justin* and that has the word *just* in it [*writing* just]. *Just* has the *ust* chunk, which makes me think of *must* and *crust* [*writing* must *and* crust]. I see *us* in *crust* [*writing* us], and I can add a letter to the *us* chunk to make *bus* [*writing* bus]. That makes me think of *plus*. (Adapted from Rasinkski, 2005.)

I ask students to underline the chunks in the words they generate in their word ladders.

Variations

Try a group word ladder. Pass a paper around the table. Each child contributes an associated word to add on to the ladder. Even more fun: time it! Give groups three minutes to build their ladder.

How about a class word ladder? Start a word ladder on a poster board, post it, and invite students to make additions!

Closing Thoughts

Building automaticity with chunks is essential to success. As research shows, "The best differentiator between good and poor readers is repeatedly found to be their knowledge of spelling patterns and their proficiency with spelling-sound translations" (Adams, 1990, p. 290). This chapter covers several methods for jump-starting students' development using the chunks in names. Now, we turn to my best lessons for supporting learners to use those chunks to strategically spell and decode. When the Significant Lessons for Guided Spelling and Decoding at the Early/Developing Levels are repeated and done in varied literacy contexts, they build students' confidence for tackling all those bigger words in their reading and writing!

CHAPTER 6

Significant Lessons for Guided Spelling and Decoding at the Early/Developing Levels

This chapter details the big-impact lessons designed to carefully guide students to spell and decode words by analogy using chunks. I call them "significant" because they involve students in explicit step-by-step processing that is key to deep understanding and application in independent reading and writing. After I shared several of these lessons at a recent workshop, one teacher provided this feedback: "Now I see how to really teach students to 'sound it out' and 'spell it how it sounds.' I realize I wasn't doing enough to teach this before. No wonder my students were having trouble. I also finally see how to put our Word Wall to good use!" I hope they'll make a huge impact on you and your students, as well!

You'll see that the lessons follow the same format as those in Chapter 4. That's because the strategic thinking is the same whether students are connecting to basic letter-sound correspondences or to chunks to help them spell and decode. If, as you review these lessons, you find you need to study examples on an easier level, see Chapter 4.

In kindergarten and first grade and with beginning English language learners, it's important to continue to make connections to your ABC Wall while working with chunks, so students still working at the basic letter-sound level are supported. For more information on using the ABC and Chunking Walls in integration, see the Masking lesson and Interactive Writing near the end of this chapter. Be sure to review the information in "Important Points Pertaining to All the Lessons" on page 67—it applies to the lessons in this chapter as well.

The Lessons

Which Name?

Which Name? is designed to guide students through the steps of connecting to names (later, other words) on the Wall for spelling and decoding. It can be done orally as a quick transition activity or extended into a fuller lesson with writing. When you're beginning to incorporate these lessons into your teaching, you might generate the words you'll work on with students ahead of time so they make connections to what's posted on your Wall. Once you get your feet wet, you'll find it's easy to come up with these lessons "on the spot."

Spelling Example

The example below is on the transitional level (Henderson, 1990; Bear et al., 2007). At this level, students are ready to work toward representing every sound within a word. This means a vowel is included in each syllable and the chunks are phonetically logical, though they may be misspelled.

As students are gathering on the carpet, I move the Chunking Name Wall front and center and begin.

Ms. Wag: We use the names on our Name Wall frequently to help us spell words we don't know. Let's practice for just a minute so you can use the Wall quickly and easily. Let's say I'm writing a letter to my mom to tell her about my trip to New Orleans. I know how to spell New (and I knew I needed a capital for the name of a place), but wasn't sure about the spelling of Orleans. Which name or names on the Wall will help me? Remember, say the word slowly, listening for the chunks. [*Provide students help with this if necessary by using a concrete model and/or clapping, feeling the jaw drop, or humming the syllables.*]

Student: *Corey* will help spell the /or/ chunk.

Ms. Wag: Yes, I hear /or/ and, you're right! *Corey* has /or/ in the first syllable of his name. So, I must need o-r. I have to remember a capital again for this proper noun. What about the last chunk?

Student: What about *Maureen*?

Ms. Wag: I hear /eeeeen/ as the chunk in *Orleans*. So, that makes me look under the /eeeee/ chunks. I see *Maureen* and hear the same chunk at the end. So, Orleans could be spelled capital O-r-l-e-e-n [*writing on the board or Magna Doodle*] and then I have to add s. Let's look at it: *New O-r-l-e-e-n-s.* What do you think, does that work?

Students: Yes.

Ms. Wag: You're right. The sounds of the chunks match up. But, the /een/ chunk is one of those chunks with more than one spelling. In this word, it is spelled e-a-n like in *bean* [*writing the correct spelling of Orleans on the board*]. O-r-l-e-e-n-s is a good, logical spelling attempt, though, and you could check your accuracy with a dictionary, spell-check on the computer, or ask an editor. Now, let's review what we did to spell this word.

Quickly review the steps you've just taken, then pose another Which Name? spelling scenario with a new word.

Use Which Name? to challenge students on words appropriate for their level in small group.

It's ideal for word work after guided reading since work with spelling affects decoding.

Decoding Example

Ms. Wag: Boys and girls, as we read, we all come across words we don't know. Let's practice what good readers do when this happens. Pretend we are reading along and we come to this unfamiliar word [*writing* investigate *on the board*]. [*Remind students to wait to read the word so everyone has a chance to practice their strategies.*] Which name or names can we connect to for help?

Student: *Sofin* has the /in/ chunk.

Ms. Wag: Yes, we use that chunk a lot, don't we? So, I know that first syllable is /in/. Anything else?

Student: /Ate/! /Ate/! Just like *Lily Cate*!

Ms. Wag: Aha! I see the last chunk in our unfamiliar word starts with the letter *a*. If I look under the *a* chunks on our Name Wall, I see *Lily Cate*. If *a-t-e* says /ate/ in *Cate*, it must say /ate/ at the end of this word. So, this syllable will be /ggggg/ /ate/, /gate/. Let's give this word a try together, starting at the beginning [*running my finger under each chunk of the word, providing support as needed*].

All: /In/ . . . [*Students pause.*]

Ms. Wag: I know the word *yes* so this must be . . . ?

Students: /Ves/!

All: /Ti/ /gate/, *investigate*!

Ms. Wag: Great job blending those chunks together to make a word! Sometimes it's funny how figuring out just one or two chunks in a word can help you read the whole word, especially if the word is in a sentence and you think of what would make sense. Let's try another.

After guiding students to decode another word:

Ms. Wag: Now, let's take just a second and go over those important steps. What did we do to read these unknown words? How will this help you as a reader?

Name Wall Races

Name Wall Races are inspired by the fact that if students can't find words on the Wall, they can't use them to make connections for spelling or decoding. When I began using Word Walls in my classroom, I assumed kids could automatically locate the words they needed. Once I realized they need support to develop referencing skills, Word Wall Races became part of our routine. Kids love to race to find words and working through the process in a guided fashion helps them use the Wall more efficiently!

Here's how it works: Two volunteers come forward to flank the Word Wall, one on each side. They are given prompts and think–time for the name they will race to find. To keep everyone active, the class also races to find the name, writing it on scratch paper or a whiteboard. On "Go!" the two racers shine their laser pointers to race for the name. The winner stays standing for another round while the other student passes the pointer to a classmate who recorded the correct name.

While a new volunteer is coming forward for the next race, we quickly debrief. "How did you find the name you needed?" "What made you look there on the Wall?" Emphasize the steps taken to quickly find analogous words on the Wall, since this is a main goal of the lesson. Focus on hearing the vowel sound in the chunk (for spelling) or seeing the first vowel in the chunk (for decoding), then looking to that vowel heading on the Word Wall. These steps really help students locate words efficiently. When they feel as though they can find words easily, they're more likely to use the Wall when they need help!

Spelling Example

Ms. Wag: We have two friends up front ready to race and you all have your whiteboards ready, right? Let's start our Name Wall Races with a word to spell. I picked up my clothes from the dry cleaner and found one of my sweaters shrank and doesn't fit anymore. Let's say I'm writing a letter requesting my money back because they ruined my sweater. If I'm spelling the word *shrank*, is there a name on the Wall that can help me? Think [*giving wait-time*]. One, two, three . . . GO! Okay, class, which of our racers found the correct name first?

All: Omar!

Ms. Wag: Okay, Omar, you're pointing to Mary Franky's name. Why?

Omar: I said /shr/ /ank/ /ank/. I heard the /a/, so I looked under the *a* chunks. I hear /ank/ in Mary Franky's name.

Ms. Wag: Exactly. You did the things a smart speller would do. First, you said the word you were trying to spell, stretching it out to hear the beginning sounds and the chunk. Then, you knew you heard /a/ so you looked there. Sure enough, *Franky* has /ank/. So, how would this word be spelled? Anyone want to try it? /Shr/ /shr/ /ank/ /ank/.

Student: *S-h-a-n-k.*

Ms. Wag: Good try. You hear the /sh/, so you started *s-h*. And, the /ank/ is easy, it's spelled *a-n-k* since we have Mary Franky's name to help us. But, if I write *s-h-a-n-k* [*writing on the board*] and run my finger under it to read it, it says /shank/. We need *shrank*. What's missing? Say it again slowly, stretching out the beginning sounds with me.

All: /Shr/ /shr/ /shr/ /ank/.

Students: R!

Ms. Wag: Right! That's a tough beginning. /Shr/ is spelled *s-h-r* like in the words *shred* and *shrimp* [*writing these on the board*]. So, we spell *shrank s-h-r-a-n-k.*

Direct students to write *shrank* correctly on their boards. The laser pointer is then passed to another volunteer with *Mary Franky* written on their board and another word is offered for the next race.

Decoding Example

Ms. Wag: Now we're going to race to find words that will help us when we're stuck while reading. After all, you have to be good at finding words on the Wall in order to use them. Remember, when I show you the unknown word, if you can read it already, don't say it! Everyone needs a chance to work on their strategies for figuring out new words, and if someone reads the word aloud, the chance is gone. Ready, racers? Everyone else ready with your board? Here's a word Lupe came across while reading about sharks yesterday [*writing the word on the board*]: *cartilage*. There's a name on our Wall that can help us read one of those chunks. Think . . . [*wait-time*]. One, two, three . . . GO! Oh, I see our racers are pointing to different names on the Wall. Nadira is pointing to *Bart* and Blake is pointing to *Charlie*. Who is right? Tell us what you were thinking, Nadira?

Nadira: I see *c-a-r-t*, so I looked under the *a* chunks. It's /cart/ like *Bart*.

Blake: But, *Charlie* has *a-r*, so I chunked the beginning as /car/.

Ms. Wag: Well, either works as long as it helps you read the word. You could say, This is /cart/ like *Bart*, or this is /car/ like /char/ in *Charlie*. Knowing this is a word in a book about sharks and using the chunk you've already read as you examine the rest of the word [*running my finger below the rest of the word*], can anyone tell me the word? Wait for five fingers!

Students: *Cartilage*!

Ms. Wag: Yes! As good readers read, they use all the clues available. I can put what I know about sharks together with the chunks I can read to figure out words. I may think something like, [*pretending to read along*] A shark's skeleton is made of /car/, /cart/, oh yes, I know—*cartilage*! Of course, good readers read all the way through the word to make sure they are correct. Yep, that fits here, all the chunks look right, and it makes sense! Since Nadira and Blake both pointed to useful names at the same time, we have a tie! Let's try another word.

Another word is offered, students race, and the class debriefs about the process.

Just for Decoding: Masking

Think of "Masking" as guided decoding. It is definitely one of the most powerful teaching techniques you can use to directly teach students how to decode unknown words. It's easy to do in all kinds of reading contexts. For this example, I've covered a word in our first-grade Morning Message using sticky notes. Notice how we use the ABC Name Wall *and* the Chunking Wall in integration. We also connect to non–name words (note how the process is exactly the same).

Ms. Wag: Boys and girls, you see I've covered a word in the Morning Message. Remember, I do this to help us

Lesson Notes

At the K–2 level, my philosophy is, it is best to encourage children to chunk words flexibly rather than bog them down with rules of syllabication. True, there are correct ways to break words into syllables. But if a child makes a connection that works, (although it is not on the by-the-book syllable break) and he ends up reading the word, he's learned to apply a very useful reading strategy! You read an example of this in the lesson above (car versus cart for cartilage). The same is true for spelling. It makes no difference whether a child chunks and spells candy as can + dy or cand + y.

practice our strategies for figuring out unknown words in our reading. Let's read the sentence together.

All: *What will your family do this _____?* [*The word* Saturday *is covered.*]

Student: *Week!*

Student: *Weekend!*

Ms. Wag: I hear some people are already using what makes sense and what fits here to predict the word. Good readers do that, but, as you know, they also use the letters and sounds in the word. If the covered word is week, what do you expect to see?

Students: *W-e-e-k.*

Ms. Wag: [*Writing* week *on the board*] If it's *week*, we'll see *w* like *Wesley* on our ABC Wall and the /eek/ chunk, *e-e-k* like the word *seek* on our Chunking Wall. I heard someone else say *weekend*. If the covered word is *weekend*, what do you expect to see?

Students: *W-e-e-k-e-n-d.*

Ms. Wag: Yes, *week* plus the word or chunk /end/ *e-n-d*. Let's take a look at the first letter in the covered word to see if it could be *week* or *weekend* [*a capital s is uncovered*]. Can it be *week* or *weekend*?

Students: No!

Ms. Wag: No, because the covered word starts with the letter *s* like *Santos*. What would fit and make sense now?

Students: *Summer!*

Students: *Saturday!*

Ms. Wag: Okay, if it's *summer*, what do you expect to see? Put your heads together with your neighbor and chunk the word. [*I lean in to listen.*]

Students share.

Ms. Wag: I heard *um* like *Umberto* and *er* like *Perla* [*writing* summer *on the board*]. Okay, if it's Saturday, what do you expect to see? Put your heads together again.

Students share.

Ms. Wag: I heard *at* like *Patrick*, *ur* like *fur* and *ay* like *Shaday* [*writing* Saturday *on the board*]. Let's uncover the first chunk now to see if either of these works. Let's reread.

All: *What will your family do this Sat . . .* [*uncovering first chunk*].

Students: *Saturday!*

Ms. Wag: I think so! There was another clue all along: the capital S. The word *summer* doesn't need a capital. [*Uncovering the rest of the word, chunk by chunk.*]

Students: /Sat/ /ur/ /day/, *Saturday!*

Ms. Wag: That fits and makes sense. *What will your family do this Saturday?* Before we talk about that, turn to your neighbor and share for a moment, what are the steps we took to figure out this unknown word?

Debrief with the class, recounting the steps.

There's real magic to the question, "If it's _____ (*students' prediction for the covered word*), what do you expect to see?" When you ask this before unmasking a word part, you force children to think through the word, segment it into sounds using phonemic awareness, and connect those sounds to chunks on the Wall. This reinforces spelling, too!

Remember, the difficulty of the lesson is easily adjusted with the difficulty of the covered word. When working with more-difficult words, though, you'll come across unusual or irregular chunks. Though the rule is to provide an analogous word if you don't have one on your Wall, at times it's appropriate just to spell the unusual or irregular word part. I covered the word *destroyed* (in the sentence: Their homes are being destroyed) from a page in a science book, by making an overhead transparency. We followed the same steps, starting with what would fit and make sense. We read on for more clues. Several students thought the word could be *ruined*. Since that has an unusual spelling, I simply wrote it on the overhead and commented about the *ed* ending. When we uncovered the first letter, *d*, students figured *destroyed* and predicted they'd see *o-y* for the chunk after connecting to the name *Troy*.

Keep in mind, you can and should mask words in multiple real-text contexts so that students see they can use these same strategies whenever, whatever they are reading.

Just for Spelling: High-Speed Spelling

This is a fast-paced, fun transition activity. I'll share two variations. The goal of the first is to review names on the Wall and build automaticity with chunks; the second involves more strategic thinking. To prepare for either, I call the students to gather on the rug, grab the Magna Doodle, and pull up the Name Chunking Wall. I choose a volunteer to come forward and take the pen of the Magna Doodle.

First variation:

Ms. Wag: Which name will you try?

Student: *Shelly.*

Ms. Wag: *Shelly. Shelly* has a useful beginning sound /sh/ and the /ell/ chunk. Ready? Go!

The volunteer quickly writes the name on the Magna Doodle, underlining the chunk. She tries to beat the time limit of five seconds. While she's writing, the class counts softly to five.

Ms. Wag: You did it! Remember, you're trying to be quick and correct, so you grow to really master those chunks. Okay, class, what words will the name *Shelly* help you read and write?

Students: *Tell, spell, spelling, smelly, telephone.*

Ms. Wag: Yes! All of those have /ell/ and are spelled like *Shelly*, e-l-l. I heard someone say *telephone.* You're right! *Telephone* has the /ell/ chunk. But, in that word, it's spelled just *e-l.* * Okay, who'd like to try to beat five seconds spelling another name and chunk from the Wall?

   ★   *Depending on the abilities of the students you're working with, you could point out how* tele *means far and is spelled the same from one related word to another like:* telescope, telegram, *and* television.

> **Lesson Notes**
>
> *Make sure students know it's okay to look at the Name Wall if needed to double-check the spelling before or as they write. Making a point of this emphasizes that the Wall can be used as a reference and that correct practice leads to mastery of the chunks.*

After each volunteer writes, be sure to ask the class to quickly generate analogous words for the chunk in the name, as in this lesson. This way, you're reviewing names and chunks and the strategy of making connections.

Second variation:

Felicia, our volunteer, is at the ready with the Magna Doodle pen in hand.

Ms. Wag: We're stuck! Can you help us spell the word *player*? [*As the class slowly counts to five, Felicia attempts to spell* player *on the Magna Doodle, underlining the chunks, beating five seconds. She writes* p-l-<u>a-y-e-r</u>.]

Ms. Wag: How did she do, class?

All: Great!

Ms. Wag: Yes, she spelled the /ay/ chunk correctly like in *Shaday* and the /er/ chunk correctly like in *Perla*. And she was quick, too! Plus, the beginning of the word was a little tricky with /pl/ spelled *p-l*. Sometimes spellers don't hear or represent all the sounds in a beginning blend like /pl/. If she spelled it with just *p* we'd have *payer* or with just *l*, we'd have *layer*. Who else would like to try to high-speed spell a word?

Lesson Notes: The words I offer for high-speed spelling are not overly challenging. The word parts are common and regularly spelled and are manageable within five seconds (you can change this to ten seconds, if needed). I save more-difficult words for the Challenge Words lessons coming up next in this chapter.

If students are struggling with this form of High-Speed Spelling, offer even easier words to try (starting with single-syllable words) and give them guidance before you start the count. For example, you might build up a student's chance for success with group scaffolding like the following:

Ms. Wag: We're stuck on the word *chilly*. Class, how many chunks are in *chilly*?

All: Two!

Ms. Wag: Let's break *chilly* into the chunks together, ready?

All: /Ch ill/ /y/.

Ms. Wag: I hear /i/ in the /ill/ chunk, so where should I look on the Wall for help?

All: The *i* chunks!

Ms. Wag: Diego, are you ready to spell the word? Go!

Incorporate the use of concrete models and provide as much guidance as needed for success.

Challenge Words

Great for opening Writing Workshop, Challenge Words engages students in using the strategies they know while providing immediate feedback for their spelling attempts. I set up the scene with something like this:

Ms. Wag: As writers, we want to use the most powerful words we can, not just ordinary words that are easy to spell. We know careful word choice makes our writing come alive. As we write, then, we all come across challenging words we're not sure how to spell. We have to know strategies for getting these more unusual words down on paper. We need to feel comfortable giving these types of words a good try. That's why we do Challenge Words lessons. They're like warm-ups for Writing Workshop, since the same steps will help you as you write independently. So, who has a challenging word they've worked on recently in their writing?

Sri: I'm writing about cyclones. I've been reading about things people can do to stay safe in disasters.

Ms. Wag: Yes, we've heard a lot about violent storms recently in the news. Sounds like Sri is using the things he's hearing about and is curious about to help guide his reading choices and his writing topics. Let's give his word a try. Before we do, let's review those good speller strategies we've been practicing. What should you do first?

Student: Chunk the word.

Ms. Wag: After you've chunked the word you should . . .

Student: Stretch each chunk out to hear its sounds and think of other words you know that have those sounds.

Student: Look to see if there are names on the Wall that have those chunks to help you spell them.

Ms. Wag: Yes, and once you've given the challenging word a try, you should run your finger under it and sound it out to see if it works. You can always try it more than once, too. Okay, let's try Sri's word *cyclone* on your scratch papers.

While students attempt the word, I walk around looking for different versions. Handing three children dry-erase markers, I ask them to go forward and write their attempts on the board.

Ms. Wag: I've asked three volunteers to come forward with three different attempts at *cyclone*. Remember, with these more challenging words, you don't have to get the spelling correct, but you need to know what to do to give the words a logical try. Let's see what we have.

I run my finger under each attempt, sounding through it as it is spelled, while providing feedback:

Ms. Wag: *C-y-k-l-n* [*spelling it aloud*]. /cy/ /kln/ [*sounding through it*].
I see the first chunk *c-y* like the word *cycle* and Mylee's name. /My/ /lee/ is spelled *m-y* so the first part of *cyclone* could be spelled *c-y* like *Mylee*. Then, I see *k-l* like *Kleenex*, so that could work for that sound, though the /cl/ blend is spelled *c-l* almost all the time. Then we have /n/. But, what about a vowel for that chunk? Remember, every chunk has to have a vowel. This is a good attempt, though.

C-i-c-l-o-n /ci/ /clon/.
Good job chunking the word and making sure you have a vowel in each chunk! First, I see *c-i*. I know the word *cider* so this could say /ci/. Next I see *c-l* /cl/. Good job spelling that /cl/ blend correctly like in the words *cling, climb,* and *cliff* and the name *Clint*! Then, there's *o-n* /on/. *O-n* says /on/ like the word *on*, so this spelling would say /ci//clon/. Hmmm . . . what needs to happen here at the end of the word so we have the right vowel sound? Let's look at the next attempt.

C-y-c-l-o-n /cy/ /clon/.

Here I see the same spelling we saw before for the first chunk, *c-y* like *Mylee*, but again, we have /clon/ like *on*. Great job remembering a vowel in the chunk, though. What do we need to do to change that vowel sound to /ō/?

I review the silent-*e* spelling pattern and make connections to the names on the Wall that follow the rule.

Ms. Wag: See, here we have *Lily Cate, a-t-e* with the silent *e* at the end to make the *a* say /ā/. Without the silent *e*, the chunk would say /at/. The same is true for *Blake, a-k-e*. Without the silent *e*, it would say /ak/. So, we need the silent *e* to make /ōne/ like in the words *bone, cone,* and *phone*—or have you ever seen this name, *Tyrone*? So, the correct spelling of *cyclone* is [*writing on the board*] *c-y-c-l-o-n-e*. Wow! That one was pretty tough! That's like a fifth-grade spelling word, guys! Good job! Let's try one more Challenge Word!

> ### Variations
>
> *In the example, I talked through each child's spelling, giving feedback. As students build skill and confidence, allow them to talk through their own attempt at the word, sharing their strategies with the class or group. Students are powerful models for each other! Then you provide feedback and reinforcement.*
>
> *If students are uncomfortable coming to the board to write their attempt, allow the class to call out their spellings. Pick a few to write on the board yourself, then proceed through the steps of the lesson. This way, the spellers are anonymous.*

Always be sure to show the correct spelling and review your purpose by debriefing about the lesson.

Lesson Notes: Notice that I've made connections to as many names on the Wall as possible to reinforce the analogy strategy. I've also offered other analogous words beyond what's posted on the Wall. When working with readers and writers in the developing stage, I think the more connections we can make, the better. I reinforce these by always taking the analogous name or word card off the Wall and tacking it above the students' spellings or, if the name or word isn't on the Wall, I always write it so it can be seen. Less experienced literacy learners receive a less in-depth analysis (see Challenge Words in Chapter 4).

Common Questions

Are you advocating incorrect spelling in many of these lessons?

I much prefer taking an active role in my students' spelling growth to giving them lists of words to memorize. Research shows that students benefit from learning spelling strategies and having plenty of opportunities to write with feedback so they can hone their skills. I started my teaching career in second grade assigning a list on Monday, practicing the words on the list throughout the week and testing on Friday. I didn't find this method effective in improving overall spelling abilities. I would much rather skillfully teach what good spellers do at different stages and give lots of opportunity to practice, practice, practice with scaffolding, guidance, and feedback.

Are these the only lessons you use to teach spelling?

No. This book has not addressed the teaching and learning of irregular high-frequency words such as *come*, *said*, and *they*. We have a small Word Wall, called the Words We Know Wall, to effectively address these. If you find your students experience difficulty with such words, you might refer to my book *Teaching Reading and Writing With Word Walls* (1999). Additionally, in second grade and higher we use a spelling log and students add their own individual words to their weekly spelling list. I detail these methods in my book *20 Tricky Writing Problems Solved!* (2004).

A combination of these methods plus constantly revisiting the significant spelling lessons makes for great success, especially in classrooms where writing workshop and writing across the curriculum are the norm. You'll see a real difference in your students' abilities to spell words in their everyday writing.

Sticky-Note Help

Sticky notes help me effectively guide *individuals* when they're stuck on spelling a word during Writing Workshop or reading a word during independent reading time.

Spelling Example

If students ask me how to spell a word, I prompt them to: say it, chunk it, sound through the chunks, and check the appropriate column on the Name Wall for any names that sound the same. I then provide help on a sticky note rather than just spell the word for them.

Student: How do you spell *transformer*?

After pursuing my usual prompts and getting no response:

Ms. Wag: We have Santos's name on the Wall with the /an/ chunk underlined [*writing* S<u>an</u>tos *or just* an *on the sticky note*]. That will help you with the first chunk. We have Corey's name under the *o* chunks with the /or/ underlined [*writing* C<u>or</u>ey *on the sticky note*]. His name will help you with the middle. Perla's name has /er/ [*writing* P<u>er</u>la *on the note*]; see it on the Wall under *e*? *Perla* sounds just like *transformer* at the end.

Depending on the situation, you might have the child try the word on the sticky note so you can further assist, or send him back to his desk to give it a try. Either way, you've prompted, provided help without spelling the word for him, and reinforced using the Name Wall and the analogy strategy!

Decoding Example

Sticky notes can also be used to help readers more easily see connections for decoding.

Hillary is reading and becomes stuck on the word *sumptuous*. After prompting her to chunk the word and think of other words she knows to help her, I continue.

Ms. Wag: Umberto's name has *u-m* [*writing it on the sticky note, underlining* u-m]. It will help you with part of the first chunk [*covering all but the first syllable of* sumptuous *with my finger*].

Hillary: *Um . . .* /s/ /um/, /sump/.

Ms. Wag: You've got it! Can you think of a word that fits here and makes sense starting with /sump/?

Hillary: No.

Ms. Wag: The next part has the u in *Lupe* [*writing* L<u>u</u>pe *on the note*].

Hillary: /T/ /u/?

Ms. Wag: Yes! Put those parts together with me [*running a finger under the word, reading*]:

Hillary and Ms. Wag: /Sumptu/

Ms. Wag: And, if this is *fabulous, f-a-b u l-o-u-s*/ [*writing it on the note*], then this is [*pointing to* ous]?

Hillary: /Ous/. *Sumptu ous, sumptuous*!

Ms. Wag: Okay, now reread.

Hillary rereads the sentence and we discuss the meaning of *sumptuous* as she reads on. In just 30 seconds, we've practiced some significant strategies!

Tying It All Together: Interactive Writing

As we finish this section on Significant Lessons and have now covered both ABC and Chunking Walls, I have to call attention to interactive writing (McCarrier et al., 1999). I make time for some form of interactive writing every day with English language learners and K–2 students by using opportunities across the curriculum. Learners grow substantially from these experiences, since they enable children to apply all they're learning. As we share the pen to write messages, reports, stories, results of experiments, letters, charts, and graphs, students listen through words for sounds (phonemic awareness). When we get stuck, we use the concrete models to guide us. Then, we refer to the Word Walls to help us spell the words we're writing. If I'm working with kindergartners, first graders, or beginning English language learners, we integrate the use of the two Name Walls. When we need a basic letter sound, we look to the ABC Wall. When we need a chunk, we look to the Chunking Wall (you'll see how this works in the lesson below). When we're done, we reread what we've written. Depending on students' abilities, we may take several days to complete something, adding just a little day by day.

Since we post our interactive writing around the room, I make sure the spellings are correct. If students come to the chart and make a mistake, we cover it with "boo-boo" tape (Post-it tape) or a "writing Band-Aid" (blank white computer labels).

Recently, during science time each day, we shared the pen for just a few minutes to write about the steps of our experiment with magnets. At the end of the experience, we drew a simple conclusion: Only metal objects can be picked up by magnets. In the transcript of the less-than-five-minute interaction below, you can see how the skills and strategies I've shared in this book all come together:

Ms. Wag: We want to write, *Only metal objects can be picked up by magnets.* I think that is a good way to state our conclusion simply. Let's first label this section of our chart, just as we've labeled the other sections. This is our conclusion. Let's see [*thinking aloud*], I need a capital for the title of the heading, a capital *C* just like Catalina's name [*pointing to the ABC Wall, writing capital* C *and the rest of the word on the chart*]. I know the chunk *sion* from the word *television*. Now, we'll start our sentence at the beginning of the next line. Only, let's see, this is the beginning of a sentence so I need a capital *O* and I hear, stretch it with me . . .

All: /O/ /n/ /l/ /y/ [*using an elastic model to segment the phonemes*].

Ms. Wag: What's the next sound?

Students: /Nnnnn/!

Ms. Wag: So we need . . . ?

Students: *N*!

Ms. Wag: Yep, *n* like *Nathan* and *Naser*. Who would like to write that on our chart? What's the next sound [*holding up the elastic model, pointing to the third piece of cardstock*]?

Students: /Lllll/!

Student: Like *Lupe*!

Ms. Wag: Yes, /lllll/, I feel my mouth is open a bit and my tongue is between my teeth, sticking out a bit like with /Llll upe/. So, we need the letter *l*. And, we can use the *y* from Shelly's name for the last sound /yyyyy/ /onl yyyyy/, /Shell yyyyy/. [*As the word is segmented, and the letters are determined, volunteers come forward to record the letters on the chart.*] *Only metal. Metal, metal . . .* help me? What's that beginning sound?

Students: /Mmmmm/ like *Mohamed*.

Ms. Wag: Yes, *m* like *Mohamed* [*handing the pen to a volunteer*]. And what's that next chunk [*using a concrete model of syllables or clapping or humming, if needed*]?

Students: /Et/!

Ms. Wag: /Et/ like . . . ?

Students: *Stetson*!

Ms. Wag: So, how do we spell the /et/ chunk?

Students: *E-t*.

I remove Stetson's name from the Chunking Wall, holding it above the chart for reinforcement as a volunteer writes.

Ms. Wag: The ending chunk in *metal* is unusual, but, what about that ending sound /lllll/?

Students: *L*!

Ms. Wag: Yep, the letter *l* as in *Lupe* again [*taking the pen and writing* a-l *to finish spelling* metal]. Let's reread.

All: *Only metal.*

Ms. Wag: What's our next word?

All: *Objects*!

Ms. Wag: Help with the first chunk.

Students: /Ob/ like *Roberto*.

Ms. Wag: You've got it! *Roberto* has the /ob/ chunk, spelled *o-b* [*holding up the name card while a volunteer writes*].

Depending on students' abilities (advanced students, late second grade), I may demonstrate how *ect* is a chunk in words like *inspect, reject,* or *suspect.* If this is not developmentally appropriate, I take the pen and think aloud to finish the word or have students join in on the /j/ and /t/ phonemes: /j/ like *Justin* and /t/ like *Tenika.*

Ms. Wag:	And what do we need for /sssss/, objectsssss?
All:	*S* like *Santos!*
Ms. Wag:	We hear /sssss/ and need *s* to show we mean more than one object. Our next word, *can,* is easy to spell. Who can spell *can*? Oh! We can use Santos's name again! /San an an tos/ . . . [*thinking aloud while handing off the pen*]. Let's reread: *Only metal objects can . . . be, be*?
All:	*B-e!*
Ms. Wag:	That's a quick and easy word we already know. [*As a volunteer writes* be,] How about *picked, picked*?
Students:	/Ppppp/ like *Patrick!*
Ms. Wag:	Yep, and what about the chunk in *picked*?
Students:	/Ick/! /Ick/ like *Patrick!*
Ms. Wag:	I think Patrick should come up and write *picked*! We need the *e-d* ending for that word. What about *up, up*? There's that /ppppp/ again!
Student:	/Up/ is like *puppy!*
Ms. Wag:	You're right! Good job thinking of a word you know to help us with that chunk. Since we don't have an /up/ word on the Wall, I'll write it for you. If this is how we spell *puppy* [*writing it on the Magna Doodle, underlining the /up/ chunk*], then how do you spell *up*?
Students:	*U-p!*
Ms. Wag:	Let's reread.
All:	*Only metal objects can be picked up.*
Ms. Wag:	. . . *by magnets.* I'll spell *by,* /b/ like *Becka* and *y* like *Mylee.* That's an easy little word. What about the word *magnets*?
Students:	*M-a-g-n-e-t-s.*
Ms. Wag:	Yep, we've written that word on our Experiment Summary chart a few times already, so it's easy to copy. That's smart spelling! *Mag* like Ms. *Wag* and *net* like *Stetson* [*running my finger under the word* magnet *higher up on the chart*]. Who'll write it for us? What do we need to end this sentence?
All:	A period.
Ms. Wag:	Right! I think we're done writing our Experiment Summary now. Let's reread the whole thing and see if there is anything else we need to add.

Finishing our Experiment Summary was a whole-group, multilevel experience. We integrated use of the two Name Walls as we worked on a range of skills from the emergent to more advanced. Though most teachers use interactive writing solely in whole-group situations, think how easily you can direct your modeling, questioning, and support to meet specific needs in small groups. Small groups can be led by an aide, parent volunteer, or even an upper-grade student. These helpers might observe you lead a few groups, making use of the Name Walls,

The CHICKS HATched.
They are TIred FrQm
peckInG ouT of their
EGGs.

Figure 6.1 *These pages were created during small-group Interactive Writing sessions with emergent writers. They were bound with pages created by other group to make a class book.*

chloe Hope chris Brad

The pirate hissed, "Ahoy mates! We are going on a treasure hunt." He showed us a map.

before leading their own. When we hatched chicks in our classroom one year, I took digital photos to document important happenings. I printed each photo on a separate page and worked in small groups for just a few minutes over several days to share the pen to write about each one. A parent volunteer helped, as well. Each sheet became a page in an informational class book that everyone had a hand in writing (though this was managed via small groups).

> ### *Lesson Note*
>
> *When sharing the pen with more developed students, I guide them through more difficult, multisyllabic words only. We can often record several sentences in one sitting.*

> ### *Hint*
>
> *Taking digital photos of class trips, events, and experiences sparks a great deal of excitement about writing. The photos make great enhancements for your Interactive Writing products.*

Another way to share the pen is by having your students work with each other in teams or pairs while you circulate to provide assistance. Remind them to use the Name Walls as needed and that their finished piece should have everyone's handwriting evident (for accountability). If mistakes are made, simply guide students to correct them using boo-boo tape or writing Band-Aids. I took pictures of a class trip to the post office, printed them out, then spread them on the floor. Everyone was asked to find a partner, pick a photo, and share the pen to write about it on a sentence strip. When we were finished, we put the sentences in order, taped them to butcher paper and made a class big book. All of this powerful literacy work was done during social studies time!

When you consider how interactive writing puts phonemic awareness and phonics skills to such good use, while creating authentic opportunities to connect to the Word Walls, you realize it's a must-do every day! Make time by employing varied grouping strategies across your content areas. You'll teach your students multiple forms and purposes for writing, and a whole lot more.

Conclusion

One of my favorite quotes, which sums up why the techniques I describe in this book are so important, came from Marilyn Adams (1990) way back when I was working on my master's degree. She wrote, "If we want our students to learn to read, we must make reading learnable for them" (p. 292). She referred to traditional rule- and worksheet-based phonics, far removed from real reading and writing, as "inherently intractable, slow (and) inefficient . . ." (p. 293). Yet, at the time, this approach was pervasive in our schools and I was living the phonics struggle every day with my second graders. It was painful to watch my below-level students laboring to sound out and spell words day after day without improvement. Then, four years later, when I moved to Washington, D.C., I found the adopted materials equally alarming. My kindergartners didn't know one letter in their names, but the phonics curriculum was a letter-of-the-week, learn-letters-and-sounds-in-isolation type, as was still the norm nationwide. Given where my students were, this didn't make sense either, especially since research demonstrates early experiences have profound effects on overall reading achievement, engagement, and cognitive development. "Children who get out of the gate quickly—who crack the spelling-to-sound code early on—appear to enter into a positive feedback loop. One of the benefits of these reciprocating effects may be a level of participation in literacy activities that leads to a lifetime habit of reading and thus sets the stage for future opportunities—opportunities not enjoyed by children who enter into this feedback loop more slowly" (Cunningham & Stanovich, 2001, p. 148). Naturally, these same effects are seen with writing. I sure didn't feel my students would be getting out of the gate quickly and easily with a letter-of-the-week, isolated approach.

These trying experiences led me to the methods I embrace today. These methods are simple, concrete, and based on common sense. In all I do, I keep application at the forefront so students use their growing knowledge in real reading and writing, thereby constantly honing their skills. Using names to grasp how sounds work in words and master letter sounds and chunks through meaningful association helps students smoothly attain goals. This approach truly makes what I'm teaching more learnable. Word Walls provide the scaffolding we need to continually use the word parts we're learning while honoring the pace of different learners. The explicit guided spelling and decoding lessons give students expert direction and feedback and the experiences they need to independently use strategies effectively. Jump-starting word and strategy learning with names makes it all kid-friendly and more fun. When you tie it together with differentiated practice, reading appropriately leveled texts, and all-day opportunities to write, you've not only made the path to literacy easier, you've made it joyous!

Appendix

Key Terms

The following terms are used throughout the book. A quick review may be helpful. Since this volume is focusing on Name Walls, I'll illustrate concepts using names as examples.

Phoneme: the smallest unit of sound in our language—the individual sound. These sound units cannot be further broken down. /m/ /u/ /l/ /h/ /ee/ /m/ are the phonemes making up the name Mulheem. Phonemes may be represented with more than one letter, as with consonant digraphs (/sh/), vowel digraphs (/oa/), and dipthongs (/oi/). There are 44 phonemes in the English language (Blevins, 2006).

Phonemic Awareness: the awareness that spoken words are made up of individual sounds. This includes the abilities to hear, manipulate (isolate, match, blend, segment, substitute, etc.) and understand how phonemes work in words. Phonemic awareness always deals with the smallest unit of sound in our language: the individual phoneme.

Phonological Awareness: This is a larger umbrella term for the awareness that spoken language is made up of sounds that can be broken down at a variety of levels. This includes the ability to hear, manipulate, and understand that sentences are comprised of words, words comprised of syllables, syllables are made up of onsets and rimes, and onsets and rimes are made up of phonemes. Thus, phonemic awareness is a subcategory of phonological awareness. The ability to match rhyming words, for example, falls under the category of phonological awareness, since it involves working with sound units larger than phonemes.

Phonemic Awareness vs. Phonics: Some teachers have confusion about the difference between phonemic awareness and phonics. They are intricately tied together, but they are distinctly different. Phonemic awareness deals with the sounds in spoken language, while phonics deals with how those sounds are represented by letters in written language. Without phonemic awareness, the understanding that words are made up of sounds, students cannot fully benefit from phonics lessons, since they don't know what the letters are supposed to represent. It's like music: how can a person learn to read and write music if he or she can't hear the sounds the notes represent? Since phonics involves how speech sounds map to letters, knowledge and facility with the speech sounds themselves is essential.

Continuous Sounds: sounds that can be sustained with an uninterrupted flow as they're voiced, like /s/, /f/, /l/, /m/, /n/, /r/, /v/, and /z/. These sounds are easier to hear, pronounce, and blend than stop sounds.

Stop Sounds: sounds in which the air flow stops, like /p/, /b/, /d/, /g/, /k/, /j/, /q/, /t/, and /w/.

Chunks: also referred to as rimes, spelling patterns, and phonograms. Chunks are the vowel(s) and the letters that follow within a syllable. As such, they are one distinct part of a syllable, or an intersyllabic unit. *Examples: en* is the chunk in the word/syllable *Ben; ev* is the first and *in* is the second chunk in the word *Kevin; er* is the first, *est* is the second, and *o* is the third chunk in the name *Ernesto,* and so on.

Onsets: the consonant or consonant cluster that precedes the vowel(s) in a syllable. So, *b* is the onset in *Ben; k* is the onset in the first syllable in *Kevin* while the last syllable does not have an onset; in *Ernesto,* only the second syllable has an onset (*n*). As you can see, syllables always have a chunk or rime, but they do not always have an onset.

Decoding by analogy: using a word part from a known word to decode an unknown word.

Decoding by analogy at the alphabet level: making connections to decode word parts by focusing on phonemes and their letter-sound correspondences (see the ABC Name Wall). For example, an emergent reader may think something like, "I know the name *Ben.* This word starts with the same letter, so it begins with /b/. I see the letter *t* like *Tineka,* so this says /t/. This must be the word *bite* because the boy in the picture is taking a big bite out of an apple."

Decoding by analogy at the chunking level: making connections to decode word parts by focusing on chunks. For example, if I know the names *Ben* and *Perla,* I can use the *en* and *er* to sound out the first two syllables in the word *en-er-gize.* The thinking may go something like, "If I know *Ben,* this is *en;* if I know *Perla,* this says *er;*" and so on. Chunks are very consistent in pronunciation and spelling from word to word, making them especially valuable to developing readers and writers.

Encoding or spelling by analogy: using a word part from a known word to spell an unknown word.

Encoding or spelling by analogy at the alphabet level: using phoneme(s) and their letter-sound correspondence(s) from known words to spell other words (again, see the ABC Name Wall). For example, if I know the words *Ben* and *Charlie,* I can connect to them to spell *beach.* The thinking may go something like, "I'm trying to spell *beach.* I hear /b/ like in the name *Ben,* so I must need the letter *b* for the first sound. I also hear /ch/ like in *Charlie,* so I must need *c-h* at the end." Developmentally, most emergent writers will hear and represent the beginning sound in words, followed by the ending sound, before graduating to hearing and representing medial sounds.

Encoding or spelling by analogy at the chunking level: using chunk(s) from known words to spell other words. For example, if I know the names *Nick* and *Perla*, I can connect to them to spell *sticker*. The thinking may go something like, "I'm trying to spell *sticker*. I hear *ick* like in the name *Nick*, so I must need the letters *i-c-k* for the first chunk. Next, I hear *er* like in *Perla*, so I must spell that last chunk the same way with *e-r.*"

Analogy strategies: I use this term when referring to making connections between words to decode and spell. Connections may be made to phonemes or rimes, as shown above, and also to syllables, onsets, and morphemes or other word parts.

Note

I don't use technical terms like onset *and* rime *with students. After all, I learned these terms when I was in graduate school! Instead, I use the kid-friendly words* chunks *or* patterns *and I refer to* onsets *as* beginning letters *or* beginning sounds within a syllable. *When talking about analogies with very young students, I use the word* connections.

References

Adams, M. J. (1990). *Beginning to read: Thinking and learning about print.* Cambridge, MA: MIT Press.

Adams, M. J., Foorman, B. R., Lundberg, I., & Beeler, T. (1998). *Phonemic awareness in young children.* Baltimore: Paul H. Brookes Publishing Co.

Allard, H. (1985). *Miss Nelson is missing!* Boston: Houghton Mifflin.

Armbruster, B. B., Lehr, F., & Osborn, J. (2001). *Put reading first: The research building blocks for teaching children to read.* Jessup, MD: ED Pubs.

Bear, D. R., Invernizzi, M., Templeton, S., & Johnson, F. (2007). *Words their way: Word study for phonics, vocabulary, and spelling instruction* (4th ed.). Upper Saddle River, NJ: Prentice Hall, Inc.

Belanger, C. (1988). *I like the rain.* Auckland, NZ: Shortland Publications.

Blevins, W. (2006). *Phonics from A to Z* (2nd ed.). New York: Scholastic.

Calkins, L. M. (1994). *The art of teaching writing.* Portsmouth, NH: Heinemann.

Cunningham, A. E., & Stanovich, K. E. (2001). What reading does for the mind. *Journal of Direct Instruction, 1*(2), 137–149.

Cunningham, P. M. (1990). The names test: A quick assessment of decoding ability. *The Reading Teacher, 44.*

Cunningham, P. M. (2008). *Phonics they use: Words for reading and writing* (5th ed.). Columbus, OH: Allyn & Bacon.

Fry, E. (1998). The most common phonograms. *The Reading Teacher, 51,* 620–622.

Good, R. H., & Kaminski, R. A. (Eds.). (2002). *Dynamic indicators of basic early literacy skills* (6th ed.). Eugene, OR: Institute for the Development of Educational Achievement. (http://dibels.uoregon.edu/).

Henderson, E. (1990). *Teaching spelling* (2nd ed.). Boston, MA: Houghton Mifflin.

Henderson, L., & Chard, J. (1980). The reader's implicit knowledge of orthographic structure. In U. Frith (Ed.), *Cognitive Processes in Spelling,* 85–116. New York: Academic Press.

International Reading Association, 1998. Phonemic awareness and the teaching of reading: A position statement. Newark, DE: International Reading Association.

Kagan, S., Kagan, M., & Kagan, L. (2000). *Reaching standards through cooperative learning: Providing for all learners in general education classrooms, English/language arts.* Port Chester, NY: National Professional Resources.

Lindamood, P., & Lindamood, P. (1998). *The Lindamood phoneme sequencing program for reading, spelling, and speech* (3rd ed.). Austin, TX: Pro-Ed., Inc.

Martin, Jr., B., & Archambault, J. (1989). *Chicka chicka boom boom.* New York: Simon & Schuster.

Mather, N., Sammons, J., & Schwartz, J. (2006). Adaptations of the names test: Easy-to-use phonics assessments. *The Reading Teacher, 60*(2), 114–122.

McCarrier, A., Fountas, I. C., & Pinnell, G. S. (1999). *Interactive writing: How language & literacy come together, K–2.* Portsmouth, NH: Heinemann.

McCormick, S. (1999). *Instructing students who have literacy problems.* Upper Saddle River, NJ: Merrill.

Pinnell, G. S., & Fountas, I. C. (1998). *Word matters.* Portsmouth, NH: Heinemann.

Rasinski, T. (2005). *Daily word ladders.* New York: Scholastic, Inc.

Slate, J. (1998). *Miss Bindergarten gets ready for kindergarten.* New York: Scholastic.

Snow, C. E., Burns, M. S., & Griffin, P. (Eds.). (1998). *Preventing reading difficulties in young children.* Washington, DC: National Academy Press.

Wagstaff, J. M. (1994). *Phonics that work! New strategies for the reading/writing classroom.* New York: Scholastic, Inc.

Wagstaff, J. M. (1997). Building practical knowledge of letter-sound correspondences: A beginner's word wall and beyond. *The Reading Teacher, 51,* 298–304.

Wagstaff, J. M. (1999). *Teaching reading and writing with word walls.* New York: Scholastic.

Wagstaff, J. M. (2001). *Irresistible sound-matching sheets and lessons that build phonemic awareness.* New York: Scholastic.

Wagstaff, J. M. (2003). *20 weekly word-study poetry packets.* New York: Scholastic.

Wagstaff, J. M. (2004). *20 tricky writing problems solved!* New York: Scholastic.

Yopp, H. K. (1992). Developing phonemic awareness in young children. *The Reading Teacher, 45*(9).

Index